THE ULTIMATE
BOOK OF
GOLF

THE ULTIMATE
BOOK OF
GOLF

DEREK LAWRENSON

MALLARD
PRESS

Half-title page: Bobby Jones, founder of The Masters

Title verso page: The 13th green at Augusta in full bloom

Title page: Nick Faldo in trouble at the 1989 Masters

MALLARD PRESS

An imprint of BDD Promotional Book
Company, Inc.
666 Fifth Avenue
New York, N.Y. 10103

Mallard Press and its accompanying
design and logo are trademarks of BDD
Promotional Book Company, Inc.

Copyright © 1991 Reed International Books Ltd

ISBN 0 7924 5414 6

First published in the United States
of America in 1991 by The Mallard Press

Produced by Mandarin Offset

*The author would like to express his special
thanks to: Simon Kellner, John Henderson and
Dudley Doust for their help during the sadly short
life of the* Sunday Correspondent; *his colleagues on
the sports desk of the* Birmingham Post *and
Vincent Kelly, the editor; those from the
Association of Golf Writers with whom he sits
shoulder to shoulder each week; to Julian Brown
and David Heslam at Octopus Publishing; and to
Gary, Linda, Paula and Marylyn.*

Jacket Photographic Credits

Front cover: All photographs supplied by Allsport/Dave Cannon except for Curtis
Strange pic courtesy of Allsport/Simon Bruty and cut-outs courtesy of Peter Dazeley.

Back cover: Main photograph courtesy of Colorsport. Cut-outs courtesy of
Peter Dazeley.

Photographic Acknowledgments

The publishers wish to thank the following photographers and organizations for
their kind permission to reproduce the following photographs:

Allsport 20, 22, 32, 34, 39, 42, 47, 49t, 55, 56, 62, 76, 79, 83, 95, 96, 128, 132, 133, 134,
136, 142, 145, 147, 165, 168, 169, 176, 185, 187b, 189/Simon Bruty 15t, 163, 173,
188/Dave Cannon 23, 41, 117, 146/Michael Hobbs Collection 141, 143b, 144t/Ken
Levine 26, 149/Don Morley 186/Stephen Munday 151/Mike Powell 11/Steve Powell
12,18t/Pascal Rondeau 140, 143t/Rick Stewart 180/Budd Symes 35/Vandystadt
85; Banff Springs Hotel 82; Colorsport 14, 28, 30, 31, 36, 38, 40b, 43, 46, 49b, 51, 59,
60, 61, 67, 68, 70, 97, 116, 137, 166; Peter Dazely 78, 94, 104, 122, 144b; Golf
Monthly 10b, 66, 159b; The Hulton Picture Company half title, 159t, 175; Japan
Golf Association 93; Bert Neale 40t, 48, 113; Tony Roberts 107; Royal Montreal
Golf Club 118, 119; Phil Sheldon title page, 9, 10t, 13, 16, 17, 18b, 19, 21, 24, 25, 27,
29, 33, 37, 44, 45, 50, 52, 53, 54, 57, 58, 63, 64, 65, 69, 71, 72-3, 74b, 75, 77, 80, 81, 84,
88l, 90, 91, 98, 99, 100, 102, 103, 105, 108, 109, 110, 111, 112, 120, 121, 123, 124, 125,
126, 127, 129, 131, 135, 138-9, 148, 150, 151t, 152, 153, 154, 155, 156, 157, 158, 160,
161, 162, 164, 167, 170, 172b, 174, 177, 178, 179, 181, 182, 183, 184, 187t; Tony
Smith 89; Bob Thomas 101; Wirtschaftswerbung Krebs 86; Yours In Sport 88t,
115; United States Golf Association/Octopus Publishing Group 171,172t.

Artwork Acknowledgments

The Publishers would like to thank the following illustrators for supplying
artwork:

Nicholas Skelton 74-75, 92-93, 108-109, 126-127
Linda Rodgers Associates/Terry McKivragan 86-87, 98-99, 104-105, 112-113,
122-123, 130, 136-137
Tony Morris 106-107, 132-133

All diagrams completed by Oxford Illustrators

CONTENTS

THE PLAYERS

PAUL AZINGER

The tours of both Europe and America are littered with players who enjoy one outstanding year, only to fall back into anonymity. So it was that when Paul Azinger was named America's player of the year in 1987 a suspicious world reserved its applause until they saw what he could come up with for an encore. Azinger's response was confirmation that here was a player with something more to offer than usual run of pro-tour clones. He was back in the winner's circle as early as March 1988 and challenging for the major championship honors that will surely come his way in the coming decade.

A British audience saw the most emphatic evidence of his burgeoning talent in the 1987 British Open at Muirfield, when he finished runner-up to Nick Faldo. Azinger admitted that inexperience of such an occasion told in the final analysis as he dropped shots

A tough and successful performance at the 1989 Ryder Cup (right) confirmed Paul Azinger as one of the world's top golfers. Below: He concentrates hard to get close out of a sand trap.

on both the final two holes to allow Faldo to win by one. But there was no dishonor in that. Every great player has been tested in such a situation before finally emerging triumphant: it is one of golf's initiation ceremonies. The trick is to learn from the experience and to benefit from it the next time such a position occurs.

All the signs are that Azinger is learning. The Florida resident, who struggled for years to combat a wild temperament and wayward hitting, was a key member of the 1989 American Ryder Cup side, and with Chip Beck formed a partnership the equal of the great Faldo-Woosnam and Ballesteros-Olazábal pairings on the European side. Indeed the two Americans defeated Faldo and Woosnam in a second day fourball when they were a mesmerizing eleven under par for 17 holes, perhaps the greatest fourball display in Ryder Cup history. Azinger capped the most satisfactory of Ryder Cup debuts by defeating none other than Ballesteros himself in the final day singles matches.

SEVERIANO BALLESTEROS

There are certain shots that are the mark of a champion. Sometimes they are strokes of sheer audacity, sometimes of nerve, and when the two combine you know you are standing in the presence of genius. Such was the feeling among those gathered around the 18th green at Royal Birkdale, Lancashire, England, one sunlit evening in July, 1976. A stunning British Open Championship was in its dying embers. The spectators had been thrilled all week by the artistry of a young Spaniard we would all hear so much more from.

Now, standing over his ball, the 18-year-old was presented with a problem. He had led after three rounds but inexperience had told and now the first prize was certain to go to the American Johnny Miller after a superlative last-round 66. But a tie for second place with Jack Nicklaus was still a possibility if only he could get down in two from the trickiest of places to which he had hit his approach shot. He was about 30 yards from the flag, but with no chance of hitting a high shot and stopping it close because the pin was cut on his side of the green and protected by bunkers.

It was time to draw from a unique well of resource. The shot he chose was a chip and run over one hump and threading it between two bunkers. Such was his deftness of touch, the ball finished just 4 feet from the flag. The audience gasped. Miller was impressed as well. Traditionally the last shot of the Open is played by the winner, but the sportsman Miller tapped in his close putt and left the stage to his young opponent. He holed his putt. Thus did Severiano Ballesteros introduce himself to the golfing world.

Fifteen years on, his place in golf's Hall of Fame is assured, and while he will fail in his desire to be remembered as the greatest golfer of all, he will leave an everlasting legacy. Lee Trevino, who knows a thing or two about manufacturing shots, once said: 'Severiano Ballesteros can do things with a golf club that no-one even thought about before, let alone tried.' To which Tom Watson, overhearing, added: 'Not even Ben Hogan.'

Learning His Craft

Ballesteros was born next door to the Royal Pedreña golf course in northern Spain, where his parents had a farm. The course was out of bounds to Ballesteros but its allure was such that he soon sought a post caddying, and during the evenings he would hone those now so precious skills on the neighboring beach. He had but one club and when there were no balls he would use pebbles. He would have chipping contests against his fellow caddies, always betting more than he could afford to lose. So did he learn not only his art

Severiano Ballesteros made his name with a short game designed in heaven. Here, at the 1987 U.S. PGA he demonstrates the art of the 30 yard pitch.

but his craft as well. For skill is never worth very much unless sharpened with a competitive edge.

From that time on, Ballesteros was always the prodigy. Aged just 10, he scored 51 in a nine-hole caddies' tournament around Pedreña. By the age of 12, whenever he was allowed to play the course, he always expected to get around at or near par.

Ballesteros never wasted much time in the amateur ranks. Indeed he was the youngest-ever Spanish pro at 16 years of age. In that first year he finished second in the Italian Open, and the following year was third in the Lancôme Trophy. After his introduction to the world stage at Birkdale there seemed little that could stop him. He topped the European order of merit for three years running and then in 1979 Ballesteros returned to Lancashire to win his first major championship.

It was very much the same mixture as before, with this time the vital ingredient of experience thrown in. But if this British Open triumph was received with rapturous applause in Britain where they now considered him one of their own, certain factions in America were less than delighted.

Welcome to the USA

The year before, Ballesteros had won for the first time on the U.S. tour, and as a courtesy gesture the commissioner Deane Beman had offered him membership without having to go through the qualifying school. Ballesteros declined. He wanted to concentrate on playing in Europe. His refusal was not well received, and now he found himself being derisively referred to in some American quarters as 'the parking lot champion' – a reference to a drive Ballesteros had hit on the 16th in the final round of the 1979 British Open, which had finished in a temporary parking lot (he still made his par!).

Ballesteros has few peers when it comes to manufacturing 'escape' shots. Here he goes again out of the rough at the Wentworth World Matchplay.

The journeyman U.S. professionals took up the theme. When he did play in the States they would greet him, in a clear act of provocation, not to mention envy: 'Morning, Steve.'

The inference was clear: Ballesteros was unwelcome in America, and his brand of play could not work there. He was a lucky winner. No sportsman is more dangerous than Ballesteros when pride is at stake. I will show them, he vowed. They will respect me.

The following year he trounced the field in the Masters at Augusta – with nine holes left he was 10 shots ahead – and with all the contempt he could muster, told the press: 'It was a lucky victory.' This win in the first major championship of the decade set the tone for 10 years when Europe would relentlessly erode the world dominance American golf had enjoyed since the early 1920s. In every sphere of the game European golfers would challenge the status quo and their chief inspiration would be Ballesteros.

Ryder Cup Hero

In 1984, at St. Andrews, he won his second British Open title by defeating the American number one Tom Watson in virtual head to head combat. The following year, Bernhard Langer would win the Masters, Sandy Lyle the British Open, and Europe the Ryder Cup for the first time in 28 years at The Belfry in England. Ballesteros would be the pivotal figure there, as he was, indeed, in both of the Ryder Cup matches that followed in which Europe emerged undefeated.

Nothing appeals more to Ballesteros than this competition. It is the classic 'us or them' situation, and honing Ballesteros's already sharp competitive edge is the memory of those early days in the United States when he felt he was not shown enough respect.

His swashbuckling play and handsome looks have been the principal reason why the game has undergone an explosive growth in Europe during the 1980s. And more major championship victories – in the 1983 Masters and in a successful return to Royal Lytham five years later – only heightened the interest. When Ballesteros is involved, events invariably take an extravagant turn. His wins at St. Andrews and Lytham, for example, were comfortably the most exciting British Open Championships of the 1980s. In the latter he closed with a round of 65, tieing the record for a winning last 18 holes in this most cherished of events. 'Once every 25 or 30 years a man gets to play that well,' he said later.

Above: Seve raises his putter in triumph during the victory at Augusta in 1980 that finally silenced the critics of the 'parking lot champion'.

Overleaf: Seve has been a major factor in the European Ryder Cup success. A 'mood' player himself, he has the ability to lift and inspire the players around him. Here he is pictured at the 1989 event.

A Talent in Decline

But there have been disappointments. The gravy train has been derailed, and never more so than in 1986 at his beloved Augusta, when, leading with four holes to play, he mishit a second shot almost in the style of a high-handicapper and it finished in the water at the front of the 15th green. That loss so affected Ballesteros that he virtually underwent a change of personality for two years. The señor lost his smile, not to mention his golf game, only for it to return, after a serious bout of self-analysis, in such wondrous fashion at Lytham.

1990 too, was disastrous, as Ballesteros was never a factor in any of the four events in which he had previously always started favorite – the major championships.

Jack Nicklaus once described a shot from a fairway bunker that Ballesteros hit at the 1983 Ryder Cup as the greatest he had ever seen. In all humility, Ballesteros said afterwards that he felt unable to agree with that assessment. In any case, as Trevino said, he has hit so many shots that everyone else could not even dream about. To claim one shot as the best would be unfair to those countless other 'Seve Specials' that set this man apart from all other golfers now playing.

MARK CALCAVECCHIA

The idea that modern American golf was devoid of personalities at the highest level was surely terminated the day Mark Calcavecchia joined the U.S. Tour. He is an Italian-American and typical of his breed. On the one hand he has a wonderfully dry sense of humor, on the other he has a temper like a powder keg, ready to explode at the first sign of his own fallibility. The one thing he is certainly not short of is personality.

He was last in the line when they were giving out the virtue of patience. During his college days he would beat out the bottom of more golf bags than he would care to remember. 'You could always tell my golf bags,' he confesses. 'They were the ones heavily taped at the bottom to stop the clubs poking through.'

Calcavecchia does not try to shape his life. He goes with the flow. He plays golf the same way. There is one famous incident at the Doral Classic a few years ago where he was playing with Jack Nicklaus in the first round. The Blue Monster, as the leading course there is known, was behaving like one, protected as it was by 30mph winds. Calcavecchia shot 65 and the Golden Bear said: 'Mark just made me feel inadequate out there. I felt intimidated in the way I suppose the younger guys used to feel when they played me. He simply blew me away.'

Calcavecchia was certainly one of those who felt intimidated when he first appeared on the circuit. Then Nicklaus, Raymond Floyd, Tom Watson and others ruled the roost. 'I was just mentally overwhelmed,' he said. The breakthrough came in 1986 when he won his first tournament, and, as so often happens, once that so important milestone was reached others proved not nearly so difficult thereafter. His introduction to the unique pressures of major championship golf proved in-

Above: Arms aloft, Mark Calcavecchia acknowledges the crowd as they acclaim his thrilling extra-time victory over Greg Norman in the 1989 British Open at Royal Troon. He still wore the smile of a champion after his defeat in the Ryder Cup later in the same year (right).

spiring when, in the 1988 Masters, it took one of the shots of the decade from Sandy Lyle to deny him the most astonishing of victories. Calcavecchia took it all in his stride. 'I have nothing to reproach myself for,' he said. 'I did not lose the tournament, Sandy wrenched it from my grasp. It will not always be that way in the future.'

Major Drama

It certainly was not. The very next year, Calcavecchia found fortune this time running in his favor. With seven holes of the 1989 British Open left, he looked destined for a top 10 spot but not really very much more. He was playing pretty mediocre golf by his own standard. And that legendary temper was fast coming to the fore when he sliced wildly his approach to the 13th hole. It was at this juncture that destiny lent a

hand. Calcavecchia thinned his recovery shot but it pitched straight into the hole. Instead of a bogey five he recorded a birdie three.

The great players seize moments like these and Calcavecchia gratefully took advantage of this most unexpected of opportunities. Now the inspiration flowed. He birdied the 16th and also the last to get into a three-way playoff with Greg Norman and Wayne Grady.

And through the first four-hole playoff in British Open history it was Calcavecchia who displayed the surest nerve. He never flapped when Norman opened it with two straight birdies. And he finished it with a five iron approach from the rough to the final hole that had the winning shot written all over it. It finished 4ft from the flag. He was to say afterwards: 'I did not care where it finished. When I saw it was

Calcavecchia is noted for his power. Here he is pictured on the 7th tee at Troon during his 1989 British Open victory.

covering the flag, I thought to myself, "do with it what you will because that is the best shot I have got".' It is an unmistakable sign of a special player that he can reproduce such shots at such moments.

Another strong indicator that Calcavecchia will leave a significant thumbprint in the game's record books is his ability to exorcise disappointment. By his own standards he failed in the 1989 Ryder Cup, but he was not afraid to admit it. Many players would have bottled up the problem and destructed for a couple of years over a bout of self-analysis. Calcavecchia just thought his play 'stank' and got on with the job. The following week he was America's leading player in the Dunhill Cup.

BEN CRENSHAW

Ben Crenshaw once said: 'I don't think I could go on living unless I felt I could win one of the major championships.' Captured in one sentence are many of the qualities of one of the more personable characters in golf: an emotional Texan in awe of the Royal and Ancient game.

His greatest strength is probably his greatest weakness. That reverence means that 'Gentle Ben,' as he is widely known, prepares more diligently than most for the four most important events of the year. But it also increases the pressure and it is probably no coincidence that a man who joined the Pro Tour with credentials as impressive as any amateur has finished runner-up or third more times than he cares to remember. At least he can go on living: he did win the 1984 Masters. Crenshaw led after the first round but going into the final day he trailed his good friend and fellow Texan Tom Kite by two shots. This was a contest between two perennial bridesmaids. Kite was known for his close finishes in the majors. So was Crenshaw, who had lost a play-off for the 1979 PGA Championship to David Graham and had finished equal second in the British Open in 1978 and 1979.

Putter Supreme

Now it was his turn for glory. Appropriately, it was his putter that gave him belief. Crenshaw, the equal of any of his generation in this department — some would argue the best of all — holed an outrageous 60ft putt on the tenth hole to set up an immensely popular triumph. Ultimately it was Tom Watson who came closest to catching him, but, ever the sportsman, he conceded: 'Ben deserved it. He has been in the hunt in a lot of major championships. This is his first and I am sure it means a lot to him.' Watson was obviously right on that score. 'There will never be a sweeter moment for me than this,' Crenshaw said.

The next year (1985) was a disaster. Most people wrote it off as a side-effect of finally having drank from the major championship well. Crenshaw knew it was more deep-seated than that. He felt tired constantly. Finally it was diagnosed as a hyperactive thyroid. Armed with the proper medication,

Crenshaw was once more challenging for honors. He reclaimed his place among the top ten players of his generation.

Given that, it seems absurd to argue that he never did fully live up to his potential. It is worth sketching in a little background detail, for Crenshaw emerged in 1973 as the hottest tour prospect since Jack Nicklaus. There

Ben Crenshaw built his reputation on the sharpness of his short game and here is a vivid example of the concentration he applied to his bunker shots in winning the 1984 Masters.

appeared no limit to what he could achieve. He had dominated college golf, and won his first tournament, the San Antonio-Texas Open, as a professional. He was just 21 years old, and he remains the youngest winner of a modern U.S. tour event, although Robert Gamez was also 21 when winning the Phoenix Open in 1990.

His fellow professionals immediately took note of Crenshaw's velvet putting touch but some were less than impressed with his 'wristy' swing action. It was true that Crenshaw was occasionally wild off the tee but given his impeccable short game it hardly seemed to matter. However, Crenshaw knew that if he became still more consistent from tee to green, there was no telling what he would win. So he embarked on a programme of trying to shorten his swing. As so often happens, when the natural instincts are tampered with, everything falls apart. Crenshaw did shorten his swing but instead of becoming straighter he became more wild. 'I ought to wear a red coat in case

As a golf historian, Ben Crenshaw would love to win the oldest major of the lot. In 1979 (above) he finished second to Seve at Lytham.

I get shot at,' he said at one point, a reference to the amount of time he spent in the trees. Only when he went back to his old teacher and his old method did the victories and the plaudits return.

One of the most outstanding examples of his innate feel for the game came in the 1987 Ryder Cup and a now notorious singles game against Eamonn Darcy. In a rare flash of temper, Crenshaw broke his putter on the 5th hole, and because it had been broken in anger he could not replace it. So now he had to putt with an implement not designed for it. He tried a wedge, a 3-iron, a 2-iron, a 1-iron. He had success with all of them. Crenshaw retrieved a three-hole deficit to stand all square on the final hole. He was eventually undone by a most courageous Irish putt, with Darcy holing a tricky 4ft putt downhill. But in defeat Crenshaw had shown why many of his peers feel the same reverence for his short game that the player does for the sport itself.

At Winged Foot, they believe in large bunkers. Ben Crenshaw appears almost a speck in the sand but at least he successfully extricated himself.

LAURA DAVIES

L aura Davies played a seminal role in the development of women's golf in Europe in the 1980s. The game desperately needed a figurehead, and her combination of raw power and understated finesse certainly fitted the bill. Within two years of turning professional she was winning tournaments all over the world. The girl from West Byfleet, in Surrey, England, began with the most important virtue, a stunning natural talent.

She could hit the ball distances rarely seen before in women's golf; and against some of her fellow professionals it meant an advantage off the tee of more than 100 yards. Clearly, when she learned to harness that power, and add to it a degree of subtlety, she would be able to mount the first serious challenge for honors by a British golfer on the American LPGA Tour. Davies's rise to fame was dramatic. In her first and second years, she topped the European money list and won the British Open. She went to America and in 1987 won the U.S. Women's Open, the highest honor in the women's game. The experts lined up to lavish praise. 'Laura can become just as good as she wants to be,' no less an authority than Nancy Lopez observed.

But perhaps it all became too easy for her. Since those heady days, Davies's career has become somewhat stuck in a rut. She has never had a lesson in her life, preferring to play the game entirely on instinct, and at times it shows, with poor course management and wayward driving. There's a little of the Greg Norman in her attitude – an all or nothing approach that attempts to bludgeon any course into submission when subtler strategies need to be applied. Sometimes the safe option, the lay up short of the water, the iron rather than a wood off a tee, is the prudent one. Also, like Norman, Davies has a penchant for fast cars off the course, and likes to bet on the horses. Given her quicksilver rise to fame, it is perhaps appropriate that she also owns a greyhound. Not 30 until 1994, she still has ample time to carve an indelible niche in the women's game.

Laura Davies is so powerful she sometimes has trouble holding on to the club with both hands. A watchful expression summarizes an extravagant but occasionally wayward talent.

NICK FALDO

A new decade brought with it a new figurehead in modern golf and for the first time it was an Englishman. Nick Faldo roared into the 1990s with victories in the Masters and the British Open Championship and the world was at his feet. Each was a glorious presentation of the qualities that make him the first name on every player's breath when it comes to talking about contenders.

At Augusta, Faldo was up against Raymond Floyd in a sudden-death play-off. The former U.S. Ryder Cup captain has built a career around a tough inner core. 'I just got intimidated by the look in Raymond Floyd's eyes,' Payne Stewart once admitted. Faldo never suffered from such feelings of inferiority. He went down the first play-off hole and made a courageous recovery from a bunker to retain an interest. And at the next, the 11th hole, it was Floyd who erred. Faldo found the green and raised his arms to the sky. The green jacket he had fought so hard to win the previous year, he had kept.

Three months later, Faldo proved beyond any question his right to be considered the best British golfer of all time with an overwhelming victory in the British Open at St. Andrews. All around the Old Course, players metaphorically doffed their caps at one who had come among them and played a game that touched the outer reaches of excellence. Greg Norman took on Faldo in the third round and got badly scarred for his pains. The result was a final round lap of honour, a triumphant tour of the St. Andrews hinterland. The five shots in hand with which he began the last 18 holes, Faldo still possessed at the end.

Yet Faldo has done all this despite being blessed with neither the natural talent of a Severiano Ballesteros nor the golfing background of a Sandy Lyle. Taking this as the context then, Faldo's story is one of the more remarkable in modern golf, exemplifying as it does the work ethic and the virtues of determination and sacrifice.

Late Starter

Faldo never even saw a golf club until he was 13 years of age. Lyle had had a 10-year head start on him. Ballesteros was already fashioning his extraordinary lexicon of shots on a beach in Pedreña. The turning point for Faldo came when he tuned into the 1971 Masters at Augusta. He did so as nothing more than a sports fan, but instantly he was intrigued by the game. Individual sports had always appealed more than team events and here he could see a pursuit where you stood or fell solely by your own efforts. In particular, Faldo was mesmerized by Jack Nicklaus. His was the face that launched a thousand golf careers and here was one more.

Faldo felt that he had no time to lose. It was the Easter holidays and the very next day he made his way down to his local club at Welwyn Garden City. There he met up with teaching professional Ian Connolly and so began a partnership that took Faldo to the brink of superstardom. Right from the start he showed a natural empathy for the game. This was despite the fact that nature had, in truth, dealt him a pretty bad hand. He was too tall for a start, and the ideal build is someone built rather stockily around the hips and backside region. But what nature had left out was compensated by his gifts as a natural athlete.

Nick Faldo surveys a shot on his way to a first major championship success at Muirfield in the 1987 British Open.

He proved the most diligent of pupils. Within three years he was down to scratch, and within four he was the English Amateur and British Youth champion. He looked an outstanding prospect. His swing, a graceful, effortless motion, drew widespread admiration.

The transition to the professional ranks proved equally smooth. In 1980, Faldo, at the age of 22, collected his second British PGA Championship title. In the British Open at Muirfield he finished 12th. In 1983 there was not a player in Europe who could touch him; he won five tournaments and had a stroke average better than any other player in the world.

A major championship victory seemed a likely sequel. That year, Faldo had been in contention in the British Open at Royal Birkdale but had faded over the closing holes. The following Spring the same thing happened at the Masters. But the general feeling was still that victories in the game's major honors would follow sooner rather than later. A first American triumph the week after Augusta, at the Sea Pines Heritage Classic, merely reinforced the feeling that Faldo was on course to collect the game's highest honors.

It was at this point, however, that both his personal and his professional life underwent drastic change. As happens to many touring professionals, Faldo's marriage failed. And then he decided that he wanted to remodel his

golf swing, having come to the conclusion that, however elegantly powerful his original swing might be, it was not totally reliable under extreme pressure. And that conclusion was confirmed by David Leadbetter, a Florida-based teacher, who told him that the swing that had earned universal admiration did, in fact, conceal serious faults. Not least of Faldo's problems was the fact that his method had become so

The 1990 British Open starts to turn Nick Faldo's way as he chips through the Valley of Sin and into the 18th hole for an eagle two.

There's no Monday morning feeling for Nick Faldo the day after winning the 1990 British Open at St. Andrews by five clear strokes.

decision to undergo swing surgery. Faldo closed out with 18 straight pars in the final round. Particularly memorable was a 3-iron second shot to the final green that never strayed for an inch from the green. If ever a shot proved the harmony of swing and golfer it was that one.

Since then Faldo has gone from strength to strength. A perfectionist, he keeps making small changes to that swing, and each time he does, he gets closer to his desired goal. He was the most consistent golfer in the world in the major championships in both 1988 and 1989, and at Augusta in the latter year he again emulated Lyle by winning the Masters.

Again, there was some startling golf on the final day. He shot 65 to tie Scott Hoch and force a sudden-death play-off. And after being handed the greatest reprieve of them all when Hoch missed from 18 inches at the first extra hole, Faldo clinched victory at the next with the most impressive of birdie threes. Here again his second shot was with a 3-iron, the sort of club which had once caused him embarrassment under pressure.

By now, Faldo had a swing that pleased not just aesthetically, but technically as well. Its imitators are legion. Faldo and Leadbetter brought out a video detailing the changes of what the former calls 'the modern swing for the modern golfer.' So successful was it that it has outstripped sales of any other sports video – a remarkable achievement for a technical work.

But then everything Faldo touches these days proves successful, because nothing is left to chance. Not many players would have switched the caddie that carried the bag in the Masters but Faldo did because he felt he needed a more ebullient personality than the quiet Andy Prodger. The result was a bubbly new caddie from Sweden called Fanny Sunesson, who is almost now a household name in her own right. And with professional contentment has come personal happiness in the form of marriage to Gill. They have two children.

Such has Faldo's personality developed and matured since meeting, and marrying his second wife that a decade that began with him petulantly bursting into tears for being fined for slow play, ended with him giving away his $175,000 first place prize money in the Suntory World Matchplay event at Wentworth, England, to a children's charity.

A sporting hero on the course had become one off it as well. And then came 1990.

A rare spot of bother for Nick Faldo during the 1990 Masters. A second successive triumph at Augusta ended all doubts as to who was the best golfer at the start of the new decade.

Major Surgery

The two years that followed were the most painful of Faldo's professional life. His decision brought general derision, which was heightened by the win of his great rival Sandy Lyle in the 1985 British Open. The critics held up Lyle as the prime example that perfect technique was not always necessary for success at the highest level. Faldo plowed on regardless. At one point, he had the Leadbetter backswing and the Faldo follow-through. But the changes slowly began to jell. And in the 1987 British Open at Muirfield, all the sacrifice proved worthwhile as he became the second Briton in three years to win this major trophy. What is more he did so in a way that fully vindicated his

habitual and ingrained that radical change would take at least two years to achieve.

Understandably, Faldo thought long and hard about that conversation. Could Leadbetter be wrong? After all, plenty of golfers in the past had won majors with serious swing faults. The trouble was, everything Leadbetter said coincided with everything that Faldo felt. He returned to Leadbetter and told him to throw the book at him.

RAYMOND FLOYD

Raymond Floyd's life reads like a twinning of two of the corniest film scripts: the archetypal rebel who came in from the cold, plus the playboy of the Western world shown the error of his ways by the love of a good woman. Who says that life does not imitate art?

Golf in the Blood

Floyd was taught the game by his father, a career soldier and later a golf professional who ran a driving range near Fort Bragg, North Carolina. Raymond's talent was obvious from the start, so much so that he was awarded the first-ever golf scholarship by the University of North Carolina. The rebel then came to the fore: Floyd dropped out after three months. He went into the army but was out of that after 18 months when he joined the U.S. Tour. It was in 1963, in his eleventh start as a professional, that Floyd won the St. Petersburg Open. He was just 20 years and six months old, the third youngest player to win on tour.

The brightest of futures seemed to beckon but the rebellious streak had quite a lot of mileage left. Floyd kept company with the wilder element and soon kept their hours and their lifestyle as well. He may well be the only tournament professional who has ever had a share in a female topless band. Simple maturity set Floyd back on the right course, and once he started setting himself goals, he again made his name for his deeds on the course.

Target Golf

In 1968 he set himself the target for the following year of a Ryder Cup berth, a major championship and $100,000 in earnings. In 1969, Floyd won three tournaments including the PGA Championship, $109,000 and played in the historic tied Ryder Cup match at Royal Birkdale.

But then good old rebel Floyd reappeared and once more he drifted until he met his current wife in 1973. Floyd had lost his desire for golf, but Maria Fraietta told him: 'If you don't want to play golf get into something else that will interest you. But stop wasting your and everyone else's time.' Floyd would later admit: 'That conversation

really shook me up.' Three years later he would have a similar effect on the field in the 1976 Masters at Augusta, when he delivered his second major championship victory by the most emphatic of nine stroke margins, equalling Nicklaus's record low aggregate of 271.

Pain for Stewart

Floyd has always been the finest of frontrunners. He is blessed with special nerve, and other players have talked about a glazed look of concentration that comes over his eyes whenever he is in contention. This was most evident in 1986 at the Open at Shinnecock Hills. Floyd was not one of the favorites for this event, simply because age was

The eye of a competitor is shown here under the Silver Pages visor. Silver dollars are more to Ray Floyd's liking and he has won them by the truckload in a career spanning four decades.

against him. He was 43, and no-one had ever won the event at that age. But the main thing he had going for him was the fact that the course at the Long Island home of the oldest incorporated golf club in the country, is one he particularly likes. He was quickly in among the pacemakers. With six holes to play, however, he trailed Payne Stewart by three shots, and his chances of finally winning the event that meant more to him than any other appeared remote.

Then came that glazed look. Stewart would later admit: 'I just became intimidated by the look in Raymond's eyes.' It turned Stewart's blood cold and with it his chances of victory. He started duffing chips, missing putts – and 90 minutes later, Floyd was the oldest winner of the national title.

Veteran swansong

Floyd's rich contribution to the American game was recognized in 1989 when he was appointed U.S. Ryder Cup captain. No man was ever prouder of the post. Floyd would call it his finest hour. He prepared for it as thoroughly as anyone. He converted a room at his North Carolina home into a Ryder Cup office where he would plot as dedicatedly as any war general what he hoped would be the downfall of the Europeans.

One of the American golf magazines even dressed him up as General Patton, the man who would restore U.S. pride. Well at times at The Belfry, Floyd looked more like General Custer, but his men ended up with an honorable tie.

And the former rebel spoke like the most die-hard of conservatives at the end, and was roundly applauded for it. He said: 'All along I have maintained that the winner must be the game of golf and it was. It is a triumph for integrity. It is marvellous for all of us.'

Just as Floyd seemed ready to head into the sunset, there was almost a glorious return at the Masters in 1990, where he was trying to become the oldest winner of the event. But the best of pacemen faltered at the end, proving that time really does wait for no man.

Overleaf: Ray Floyd steers another putt towards the cup during his sensational US Open win at Shinnecock Hills in 1986.

ROBERT GAMEZ

As stupendous a performance as it was, there had been other players before Robert Gamez who had emulated his achievement of winning his first event as a professional. All had suffered some sort of reaction thereafter as the instant acquisition of fame took its toll.

There were some critics then who took this as their lead-off point when referring to Gamez and refused to recognize that a prodigious talent had come within their midst. 'Let's see how long it takes him to win again,' they said. 'Let's see if he can win an event with a stronger field.'

One American magazine ran a feature on the problems for rookie professionals in trying to live up to such early fame. Before it had hit the streets, the 21-year-old Gamez had rendered it pointless. In his ninth event in Orlando, Florida, he had won again, and this time an event described by its instigator, Arnold Palmer, as boasting 'the strongest field in world golf this year.' Palmer had a point. The Bay Hill International entry had all the leading Europeans, as well as all the best Americans. As the tournament reached its climax, all were headed by the Australian Greg Norman. But on the 18th, rated statistically the toughest on the U.S. tour, Gamez, one shot behind, demonstrated his innate ability to make things happen. This had first been seen publicly the previous year when he holed a 30ft putt on the final green to win his Walker Cup singles match against the Briton Stephen Dodd.

Now his 170-yard 7-iron second shot flew over a dangerous expanse of water that protected the pin, bounced in the 15ft that separated flag from hazard, and then dropped into the hole for an eagle two. The subsequent roar must have been heard 200 miles away in Miami.

At St. Andrews in July, Gamez was at it again. His first trip to Britain, his first appearance in a British Open. Yet within five holes of his first trip round the most mystifying of all courses, Gamez had had two eagles. He went on to finish 12th. All of which establishes a strong link with greatness. The young man from Las Vegas has Mexican antecedents and it is not surprising that he refers to Lee Trevino as his soul brother. The finest compliment that can be paid in return is that Gamez appears to have what it takes to go on and rival his soul brother's achievements.

Gamez leaps for joy after holing a 30ft putt to defeat Stephen Dodd on the final hole of their Walker Cup singles match in 1989.

WAYNE GRADY

The year 1990 produced two predictable major championship successes and two surprises. The former belonged both to Nick Faldo. The latter went to Hale Irwin and a genial Australian, Wayne Grady.

When the 33-year-old from Brisbane lost the British Open at Royal Troon the previous year to Mark Calcavecchia in a four-hole play-off, a great many people expected to hear no more from him in the game's premier events.

After all, this is a man whose career has been dotted with no less than 29 runners-up finishes. Grady had led the British Open for a good deal of its considerable length and to ultimately fail appeared to indicate a missing piece as far as making up a major championship jigsaw was concerned.

Grady's chance to silence such talk came in the PGA Championship at Shoal Creek. Like the British Open, he led after the second and third rounds. Indeed, when he was headed by Freddie Couples with six holes to play, the script appeared to be reproducing itself with cruel accuracy.

But no less a judge than Jack Nicklaus predicted that Grady would not defeat himself and so it proved. It was Couples who stumbled with late bogies to lose the lead. It was Grady who lasted the distance.

Grady did not play golf until he was 14. His first love was aeroplanes and he wanted to be a pilot. At least in today's jet-setting golf world, he can continue to satisfy his lust for having his head in the clouds.

In 1984, Grady won the German Open but it was not until 1989 that he won on the U.S. tour, in the Westchester Classic. That event proved the making of him. A few weeks later came his performance in the British Open, and the year closed with a memorable victory for himself and Peter Fowler when representing Australia in the World Cup.

Grady's victory in the PGA Championship elevated his career a further notch. A year that began with one Australian, Norman, making waves in America, ended with another causing a far greater splash.

Life as a perpetual runner-up came to an end for Wayne Grady in 1990 and it was chiefly because of his ability to hole putts of this range.

HALE IRWIN

If Hale Irwin had gone into a telephone booth and come out wrapped in a Superman costume, his image could not have undergone a more radical change than that which greeted his return to the public eye in 1990.

Throughout the 1970s and early 80s, the bespectacled Irwin presented a studious approach to the Royal and Ancient game. He looked as, if he was taking time off from managing a bank, and very successfully too.

Few players were more admired for their competitive instincts. And due to a virtuoso shotmaking ability, Irwin won tournaments on what are traditionally thought of as some of America's toughest courses. It came as no surprise when he prevailed in two U.S. Opens, the first at Winged Foot, New York in 1974 and the second at Inverness, Ohio in 1979, which are traditionally played on tigerish layouts. And between 1975 and 1978, Irwin went 86 tournaments in America without missing the halfway cut – the third longest sequence in U.S. tour history.

But Irwin was a forgotten man as the final decade of the 20th Century began. The observant may have noticed that he had shed the glasses in favour of contact lenses. At 44 he seemed to have shed the skills as well that had made him such a household name. The previous season he had finished 93rd on the U.S. money list, his worst since his opening year on tour, way back in 1968.

Just as the golfing obituaries were being written however, Irwin got up and danced a fantastic jig on his own grave. At the 1990 U.S. Open at Medinah, he rediscovered how to play the game, and at the 72nd hole he sank a 40ft putt that got him into a play-off.

One could well have imagined the old Irwin raising his arms briefly in the air after such a feat and then quickly folding them again, embarrassed by such a show of public emotion. This Irwin did a lap of honour around the green. He 'high-fived' every member of the public who was in range. And then, just for the press who had not witnessed it, he did it again in the media tent. It was *the* moment of 1990, and it all recalled the days of his youth, when he was a star defensive back for the University of Colorado's football team. Irwin went

on to win the play-off at Medinah against Mike Donald, and so joined an élite group of names indeed who have won that illustrious trophy three times. And just in case anyone thought it was a fluke, Irwin went out and won the Buick Classic as well the very next week. Clearly the obituarists will have to wait a while longer before penning their copy.

Hale Irwin, before he discovered the virtues of contact lenses. Irwin was renowned for a steely eye behind those metal frames and it brought him a place among the elite.

TONY JACKLIN

In some people, heartbreak and happiness are twin imposters that fight a never-ending battle for control over their personal and professional lives. In no golfer is this more strikingly apparent than Tony Jacklin. Whenever Jacklin is not enjoying the sweetest of moments it seems he is undergoing the bitterest. In his playing career, he took British golf to heights unknown since Henry Cotton's heyday. He won the British Open and the U.S. Open in the space of 11 months. He seemed on the threshold of world dominance. But fate decided enough was enough, and put on the brass knuckles: Jacklin never won another major.

Some years later, just as Jacklin was contemplating retirement as Ryder Cup captain to spend more time with Vivienne, his wife of 20 years' standing, she suffered a shocking brain haemorrhage and died.

Jacklin, awkward and rebellious like Cotton in the 30s, transformed the British golfing scene. The son of a Shropshire truck driver, he was cocksure and arrogant, knew exactly what he wanted and knew he had the skill, the talent, and the dedication to get it.

His liking for colorful clothes (witness the mauve outfit in which he won the 1969 British Open) and disregard for the most cherished traditions endeared him to few of the old school.

But British golf at the time was shedding its elitist traditions and as the game developed in new areas of society, so these new followers found their perfect role model. And how Jacklin loved it. For many the burden of a nation's expectations is intolerable but

In 1969 Tony Jacklin at last ended an extended spell of overseas domination of the British Open with a memorable victory at Lytham.

Jacklin took it all in his confident stride. And why not? The boy could play, like few others before or since. He had a swing made in heaven and an attitude priceless to those who want to succeed.

Early Success

By 1966, while still only 22, he had topped the European order of merit and been selected to represent England with Peter Alliss in the Canada Cup (now the World Cup). He was invited to the 1967 Masters and led briefly in the third round.

Jacklin looked around him and knew that if he wanted to be the best, he would have to compete more often with them. So he played full-time on the U.S. Tour and in the time-honored tradition, the run-of-the-mill American professionals made him about as welcome as a cat in a doghouse. Jacklin spent nights in lonely hotel bedrooms but channeled his frustration into winning tournaments. He claimed the 1968 Jacksonville Open and then two years later, became the first British player for 18 years to win the British Open. He did it in the style that became his trademark. He kept a six off his card for the whole championship and saved his best stroke for the very end, a superlative drive threaded through the treacherous bunkers on either side of the 18th that is still talked about.

Hazeltine Humbled

Jacklin merely banked the success and strove for more glory. The U.S. Open the following year was played on a heavily

criticized course in Minnesota called Hazeltine. 'What does it lack?' someone asked the outspoken U.S. professional Dave Hill. 'Eighty acres of corn and a few cows,' was his caustic reply. He was not the only one who was psyched out. Of the 150 who started, 69 shot 80 or more on the first day. Jacklin, meanwhile could hardly contain his excitement. He just laughed aloud at

Knee deep in rough (above) Tony Jacklin peers anxiously after his ball. It was an expression seen time and again during his years as Ryder Cup captain (left) but it would be replaced by a triumphant grin as Europe learned to compete with American excellence.

A thoughtful captain, Tony Jacklin considers team tactics during practice for the 1989 Ryder Cup which was held at the Belfry in England.

the criticism. He could see nothing wrong with the course, and proceeded to shoot 71-70-70-70. Jacklin won by no less than seven shots. He had become the first British player for 50 years to win the Open and in doing so had trounced the Americans, Nicklaus, Palmer and all, in their own backyard. Happiness hardly comes in bigger portions. But heartbreak was waiting just around the corner.

Jacklin made the most electrifying start possible to his British Open defence in 1970 at St. Andrews. He went out in 29 strokes. He could do no wrong. He holed chip shots, putts that took three borrows, you name it. But on the inward nine, a thunderstorm broke and with Jacklin still five holes from home, play was suspended for the day. He returned the next day, but the magic did not. A likely 63 became a 67, and Jacklin was three shots adrift at the end.

The following year he finished two strokes behind Lee Trevino, but in 1972 at Muirfield, it looked certain that the Mexican would be handing the trophy back to his English opponent. On the next to last hole, as Trevino hacked his way down the left, he even said: 'That's it. I have thrown my

title away.' Then up popped fate to lend a hand. Trevino chipped in, just as he had on countless occasions over the previous 34 holes. Jacklin had started the hole one adrift, looked all the way through it as if he would go one ahead, only to fall an irrevocable two behind going to the final tee. Who can fathom this great game?

Certainly Jacklin could not after that date. He was never really the same player again. The man who had contended strongly in six consecutive championships was never closer than 13 shots to the winner from that date on. The fans would still turn up, even 17 years later, in the hope of one authentic last glimpse of the legend. But it never came, and the sight of Jacklin going into the 1989 British Open at Royal Troon with a putter fitted with something resembling a broom handle for a shaft must have been the final straw.

Ryder Cup Revivalist

But he remained at the center of people's affections in his role as Ryder Cup captain. Jacklin took on the job in 1983, and insisted from the start that everyone in the party travelled first-

class and stayed in the finest hotels. As ever, he did things his way. He believed that if you treat people as second-class citizens they live down to your expectations.

Well, Great Britain and Europe lost by one point that year but they were never to lose again during Jacklin's glorious six-year reign. He gained some measure of compensation for earlier events by defeating Trevino's team at The Belfry in 1985, and then led Britain and Europe to an historic first success on American soil two years later. That was at the course Jack built, Muirfield Village, Ohio, when the man himself, Nicklaus, was captain. In 1989 the match that was now being hailed as one of the great sporting occasions ended in a tie. Jacklin said his farewells, knowing he had played his part in an unparalleled expansion of the game throughout Europe. Just as he had all those years earlier as a player.

TOM KITE

Golf has brought Tom Kite more prize money than any other player alive but it has not brought him a proportionate amount of fame. By the time he was 40, Kite had become the first man to earn over $5 million in tournament winnings: but money does not buy you happiness. The amiable man from Texas once threatened to quit the game because he did not win often enough. And while that day is long since forgotten, one looks at Kite's record of just 13 tour victories in his first 18 years on tour and the verdict has to be: yes, he does *not* win enough.

Why? His detractors reach straight for the knee-jerk reaction. He 'chokes' down the home straight, doesn't he? Time and again Kite has been in position to win a major championship only to blow it over the closing holes. It looked as if he would put the record straight in the 1989 U.S. Open when he led by three strokes with 15 holes to play. But three shots is not so big a lead at that stage, especially for someone who has still to land one of the game's four most coveted prizes. Kite ran up a triple-bogey eight at the 5th. He never even finished in the top five.

Yet if this pressure thing kills him every time, why does he not fold similarly in the Ryder Cup? There, the players who know, reckon the nerves jangle even more destructively than they do in the majors: not only is your own 'life' at stake, but that of your compatriots, your country even. In the Ryder Cup, Kite is as rock-solid a character as you would ever want on your side. In six appearances in this event he has still to finish on the losing side in a singles game. In 1989 at The Belfry, he demolished the hapless Howard Clark by 8 & 6. And in 1981 at Walton Heath, England, in perhaps the finest Ryder Cup singles ever, Sandy Lyle, his opponent, had eight birdies – yet lost 3 & 2.

Career High

If ever a year could be used as a summation of Kite's career it was probably the last one of the 1980s. For most of the

year, Kite did as kites do. He flew high. He won the order of merit, he won two prestigious events, he won pots of money. One of those wins came in The Tournament Players' Championship, when he defeated one of the best fields of the year. The other came in the season-ending Nabisco Championship. Fittingly for the $5 million man, that triggered all sorts of cash bonuses. But Kite would probably have given it all away just to have hung on and won the U.S. Open. It is no disrespect to Curtis Strange to say it is a shame in many ways that he did not. For what we can say, without a shadow of a doubt, and whichever side of the fence you stand on as to assessing Kite's

He may stumble in the major championships but representing the USA in the Ryder Cup has always brought the best out of Texan Tom Kite.

Kite explodes out of a St. Andrews bunker during the USA's 1989 Dunhill Cup win where he was partnered by Calcavecchia and Strange.

worth as a player, far worse golfers than him have tasted victory in a major.

Kite began playing golf at the age of six, when his father in Austin, Texas, put a club in his hand and urged him to give the game a try. By the age of 11 he had won his first event and he went on to win Walker Cup honors. In 1981 he finished number one on the money list, and there began what seemed to be an inevitable progress towards becoming one of the game's great players.

But as the years slipped by, so did the major championships. He seemed to be in contention just about every year of the decade to win the Masters, but always the putts failed to drop at the required moments. Similarly, he had his chances in the U.S. Open and the British Open Championships. Maybe in another lifetime, Kite will come back and win the Grand Slam. Now, he is just the holder of a money title and even that will be pretty meaningless in 10 years time if the victory purses keep on spiralling at their present rate.

For all that, Kite wears with good grace the unenviable burden of being known as the best player never to win a major.

BERNHARD LANGER

Most of the profiles of players in this book illustrate the pivotal role that indomitable will plays in the make-up of every top athlete. But of all the top golfers featured here, none has had to show as much of it as the German Bernhard Langer.

Langer began playing the game at the age of nine and quickly matured. Ironically, in view of what was to befall him, it was his putting skills that first shone through, only to be let down by an erratic long game. But with an appetite for practice that has never left him, Langer eradicated those faults, and when he first emerged in 1976, his consistency to the green quickly took the eye. Not half as much, however, as what happened when he got there. For on the greens, Langer was a total mess. The empathy he had demonstrated for this side of the game as a youngster had now deserted him to such an extent that grown men turned away from watching him lest they should also become so 'infected.' Langer had the dreaded golfing disease known as the 'yips' and he had it badly. It would have finished a lesser man there and then, but after an 18-month hiatus while serving in the army, Langer developed a putting stroke in his spare time that he thought would work. The army matured him, and it was a much more confident individual who emerged. Langer spent endless hours on the putting green making his new stroke habitual. And, glory be, it did work. He won three times in 1983 and in 1984 was as good a shotmaker – especially with the long irons – as any player in the world. Severiano Ballesteros may have won the British Open at St. Andrews that year but if Langer's old nemesis, dodginess on the greens, had not reappeared on the final day, Germany might have been saluting its first victory in the event.

Master Craftsman

The Germans did celebrate their first Masters win the following year. The dream that Langer had worked so hard to attain had been realized and how rewarding it was to succeed at Augusta, home of the trickiest greens in the world. Langer only had one three-putt in 72 holes and defeated Bal-

Bernhard Langer shows his ability to improvize in any situation during the 1981 Benson and Hedges International Tournament in England.

lesteros into the bargain. His world-class status was assured when he won the Heritage Classic the following week, and now the extent of what he could achieve seemed limitless.

In 1987, Langer won the British PGA Championship at Wentworth and the Irish Open with two displays of golf that will never be forgotten by those who witnessed them. After the first, Ballesteros said charitably: 'Bernhard probably played the game as well as it

can be played this week.' Ironically it was on the same course 12 months later, that Langer would witness the return of his worst nightmare. Defending his championship, he had led after two rounds, but for the last 36 holes he endured a horrid time on the greens. The 'yips' had returned. He five-putted one green during a last round 80 in the 1988 British Open at Lytham, and it was the saddest of sights to see one of the most determined and amiable of golfers reduced to that.

Langer made pitiable viewing all year but typically he never gave up. He read every book on the subject, his attractive personality meant that he got thousands of letters on the subject. All wished him well. Langer read every one of them, and tried out all the theories.

Eventually he re-emerged in 1989 with the weirdest of methods, his left thumb clamped across his right wrist to provide support. Miraculously, there was a return to form of sorts. Langer won the Spanish Open and his native German Masters and played well enough to qualify for the Ryder Cup without having to rely on a favor from Tony Jacklin.

His golfing record alone would earn him folk status in his native land, but his dedication means he has admirers wherever the game is played and, in Germany, even among people who have never set foot on a course. In return, Langer has put his name to efforts encouraging golf in his homeland, and is designing courses. One way or another, whatever fate has decreed for him in the future on the greens, he will not be forgotten.

The laid back approach! Langer celebrates an important putt during the 1987 Ryder Cup.

NANCY LOPEZ

They say the British public are not very interested in ladies' golf, but they recognise a superstar when they see one, whatever the sex. And they warmed to Nancy Lopez from the start when she made a sensational first appearance in Britain in 1977.

The previous year Britain had been thrilled by a young Spaniard with dashing good looks and a game to match. Now here was another Latin of similar style and panache. Severiano Ballesteros and Lopez. It was almost too good to be true. And while Ballesteros galvanized the sport throughout Europe, Lopez played a similar role on the LPGA tour. Lopez won that first British event, the European Open. Indeed she won just about everywhere that year. It was her rookie season and she ended it with a hatful of titles to her name. She had it all. She had one of the smoothest putting strokes in golf, and on the rare occasions when everything failed to mesh, she would toss back her mane of black hair and smile. In one season, the name of Lopez had become synonymous with women's golf.

Many players have found a successful first season hard to follow, but Lopez's answer was a sequel year that produced still more victories. Once more no-one could touch her. After two years on the scene, she had won 17 times.

Leading Amateur

Lopez was born in Roswell, New Mexico, to parents with a lifelong love of the game. Her father, Domingo, who ran a car repair business, was an accomplished low-handicap player and in the time-honored fashion, it was from visits to the local club that Nancy developed her enthusiasm for the game. From the outset she demonstrated precocious skills. She was only 12 when she won the state amateur championship. Twice she won the United States Golf Association Junior Championship, but it was in the 1975 U.S. Women's Open, when just 18, that Lopez turned a few heads: still an amateur, she tied

Nancy Lopez's grace and beauty have established her as the most instantly recognizable woman golfer all over the world.

for second place just four shots behind the winner, Sandra Palmer. (Extraordinarily, in view of what she would go on to achieve, second remains the best finish that Lopez has ever registered in the most prestigious event in the women's game.)

Despite that astonishing performance, Lopez had no desire to rush into the professional branch of the sport. The following year was a Curtis Cup one, so she remained an amateur for that, and finished up being named Tulsa University's female athlete of the year.

The pressure now to move into the paid game was proving too great. She did not complete her university studies, but turned pro after her sophomore year. What for many would have been a reckless gamble was a sure-fire

Nancy Lopez plays an approach during the 1989 LPGA tournament in San Jose, California.

certainty in this instance.

Lopez finished third at the LPGA qualifying school, and then came those momentous opening two years. In her fourth and fifth starts on the tour, she was a winner.

Lopez did not dominate the 80s quite as decisively as the experts had predicted. There was a broken marriage with which to contend, and then, after re-marriage to the baseball star Ray

Knight, she took time off to have two children. When she returned the LPGA had moved on: the new standards that she herself had set had been taken up by a new generation inspired by her example.

But although her aura of omnipotence had certainly dimmed, we should keep Lopez's 'decline' in perspective. She still won – often. In 1985, for example, there were five more wins in a year when she set a new record stroke average of 70.73. Lopez was Player of the Year once more. There were other landmarks. In 1983 she ex-

ceeded $1 million in tour earnings, and then some years later became only the second player, after Amy Alcott, to break the $2 million barrier. But perhaps the greatest honor was also the most inevitable. At the first opportunity, Lopez became the 11th inductee into the LPGA Hall of Fame. The LPGA handbook lists this as one of the most 'difficult attainments in today's sports.' Once more, everything is relative. When you've been blessed like Nancy Lopez, such an attainment becomes nothing more than just a natural progression.

SANDY LYLE

When Tony Jacklin won the 1969 British Open at Lytham, there must have been a thousand excited 11-year-olds who turned to their fathers and said: 'I'll do that one day.' Sandy Lyle was one of them. The difference was, in his case, that he went out and caught the dream. Even at such a tender age, there was more than an inkling of what lay ahead. Legend has it that at the age of three, Lyle's first shot flew 75 yards. By the age of eight he was playing 18 holes regularly. And by the time he witnessed Jacklin's historic triumph he could see his future path laid out before him.

Golf in the Blood

Lyle then, was born to play professional golf. His father, now retired, was the club professional at Hawkstone Park in Shropshire, England, and Lyle would practise there, morning and night, learning the parental dictum: tempo, not temper. As soon as he was in his teens he was playing for a county team, and at the age of 16, the next time the British Open was at Lytham, Lyle was a competitor, not a spectator.

Arguably the finest natural talent that the British game has yet seen, he was now on full display. Lyle was already hitting the ball stupendous distances, and cleaning up on the amateur circuit. In the next three years, he twice won the English Amateur Strokeplay Championship (the Brabazon Trophy) and was selected for the 1977 Walker Cup. His introduction to the professional ranks was no less dramatic. Lyle won the European tour's qualifying school and a tournament in his first year.

Go West Young Man

By the age of 22 he had twice topped the order of merit and played in the Ryder Cup. There he met up with Jacklin, and the voice of his mentor was a persuasive one as Lyle decided, just as Jacko had before him, to play full-time on the United States tour. That was where Lyle's career went, for the first time, into reverse gear. In Europe a magnificent long game compensated for some inadequacies in his short game. In America no such luxuries could be afforded. For a start, in 1983, the competition was 10 times tougher. For another, all the greens were protected by a collar of rough and so any shot that erred a fraction meant the most delicate of chips was necessary to have any chance of saving par. It was a shot Lyle did not possess. Neither did he prosper on the much faster greens. It says much for his perseverance, a quality he is not always given credit for, that five years later he was recognized as a player

Sandy Lyle stamped himself on the modern game by becoming the first British winner of the Masters and the first for 16 years of the British Open.

possessing exceptional touch and feel.

But before success in America, there was success back home. Lyle kept his promise to his father in 1985 when he won the British Open at Royal St. George's. All Britain celebrated like they had not since the last British win that had had such a profound effect on a young Lyle. What made the success the more appealing was Lyle's modest nature. He was unassuming almost to a fault. A reporter almost blanched when he asked Sandy whether the win would change his life. Well, it made him a millionaire but not one who would go around boasting about it.

Lyle kisses the coveted silver claret jug awarded to winners of the British Open after his win at Royal St. George's, Sandwich, in 1985.

If Lyle will always cherish the first half of the decade for the achievements he compiled in Europe, the second half will cause him to recall America with affection. In 1986, he claimed his first U.S. tour title, the Greater Greensboro Open, to be followed 12 months later by the prestigious Tournament Players' Championship in Florida, the event American professionals like to think of as the 'fifth major.' In the fall of that year, Lyle teamed up with Bernhard Langer to form a pivotal partnership in a historic European Ryder Cup triumph on American soil. Three times the captain Jacklin paired them together in Muirfield Village, Ohio, and on each occasion they came up with the necessary point.

Lyle was now fully established in America but what happened the following spring will ensure him his own special place in golf lore.

For the first three months of the year, as he trailed across America's Southern states, Lyle could do no wrong. By the middle of April he had won over $650,000 dollars, but the money was irrelevant alongside the pride that came with becoming the first-ever British golfer to wear the coveted green jacket that goes to the winner of the Masters.

History in the Making

Lyle went into the event as one of the favorites, but history was not on his side. Not only had Augusta proved a barren venue for British golfers, but Lyle had won the Greensboro tournament the week before, and no golfer had won the event that leads up to the Masters as well as emerging triumphant in the event itself. Lyle shooed away superstition. He had also won the Tucson Open, and knew that Augusta National, favouring as it does the big hitters, was made for him. And now he had a winning style to fall back on as well.

He began imperiously. He was leading after 36 holes, and going into the final round appeared well nigh unstoppable. But the pressure of being front man for so long told at the treacherous short 12th where he put his tee shot into the water. Now he had fallen behind the talented Mark Calcavecchia. If he was going to win, he would have to do so by the hardest method of all. That he did so is now history, as is the way he managed it. His 7-iron from a fairway bunker on the final hole which led to the winning birdie is acknowledged by the distinguished golf writer, Herbert Warren Wind, as the greatest sand shot in the history of the game. Lyle returned home to Europe

and cleaned up there as well. He won the Dunhill Masters at Woburn, and then (having lost four previous finals) the Suntory World Matchplay Championship at Wentworth.

Perhaps a reaction to all this success, unprecedented in a British golfer, was inevitable. For much of 1989 and 1990, Lyle cut a sad figure, totally at odds with the game, as his great rival Nick Faldo collected all the trophies he had striven so hard to win. At least he had

A thoughtful Sandy Lyle considers the results of a chip shot from a sloping lie during his 1985 British Open win.

the consolation of knowing his name was on those trophies first. And that the dream he had cherished as an 11-year-old in a wind-swept grandstand at Lytham had not only come to pass but had proved merely the opening frames in a glorious picture that should run for some time yet.

JACK NICKLAUS

Nothing more vividly illustrates Jack Nicklaus's impact on his chosen sport than the fact the 'Golfer of the Century' is already known and inscribed in lore even though the Millennium is still merely a dot on the horizon. Nothing that happens between now and the year 2000 can mask the great man's omnipotence. Severiano Ballesteros, for example, could win a major championship every year between now and that date and still not have accumulated as many as the man known as the Golden Bear. Golden is right: sprinkled liberally over a playing career spanning three decades have been six Masters titles, five PGA Championships, four U.S. Opens, three British Opens, and two U.S. Amateurs. And yet that extraordinary list of achievements merely tells the half of

Above: Caddie Jimmy Dickinson with Jack Nicklaus during the 1966 Open at Muirfield. The partnership has been one of the most lasting in golf. Left: Jack lets it rip during the 1970 British Open at St. Andrews.

the Nicklaus legend. Just as staggering is the number of times that he was in contention and did not win. He was runner-up on no less than 58 occasions, including seven times in the British Open.

Gentleman Jack

While anyone can be magnanimous in victory, it is the way Nicklaus accepts adversity that enhances his reputation. Two chapters from his glorious career provide examples. One came from the part he played in perhaps the greatest British Open of them all, in 1977 at Turnberry, Scotland, when he and Tom Watson duelled over the last 36 birdie-laden holes. Here we had the two greatest players of the day performing pretty much at the peak of their powers. No-one else could live with them. Hubert Green was third, no less than 11 shots behind the winning score. In the third round both men shot 65, to be tied going into the final 18 holes. For much of the day, Nicklaus had a one-stroke lead. But that evaporated at the short 15th, where Watson holed an outrageous putt of fully 20 yards. At the 17th Watson went in front for the first time when Nicklaus missed a 4ft putt. Watson held on for victory, matching Nicklaus's birdie at the last, and while he prepared his victory speech, the vanquished had to digest the fact that he had shot 65, 66 and lost. Imagine the disappointment of someone with an insatiable lust for victory to play so well and come away empty-handed! But Nicklaus instantly overcame his anguish. He put his arm round Watson, in fact it looked as if he would never stop congratulating him. The two had drawn from each other performances of staggering virtuosity and Nicklaus, peering through the mist of disappointment, had recognized a kindred spirit.

He did so as well in the 1969 Ryder Cup. Then the worthy who was up

With such gestures, Nicklaus, more than anyone, helped maintain the standards of behavior in golf that are still prevalent today, and which many other sports have allowed to rot. But while Nicklaus could lose gracefully, let us not lose sight of the fact he also could win better than any man as well. Nicklaus possessed that ability from the start. He began playing the game at the age of 10, and 12 months later he shot 81. Twelve months on, and he broke 70 for the first time, holing a 30ft putt across a wet green in semidarkness for an eagle three.

Junior Prodigy

The titles, naturally, flowed as well. At 13, he was the Under-15s Ohio junior

A rare picture of Nicklaus in trouble on his favorite course, Augusta. The following year he won the Masters for a record sixth time.

against him was Tony Jacklin, who stood over a 3ft putt on the final green in his singles match, knowing it was not only for a tie with Nicklaus but a tie for the whole match. If he had missed it, the man who had tasted the sweetest of victories just months earlier in the British Open at Lytham, would have been staring at the sort of misfortune that can scar a man for life. While all this ran through Jacklin's mind, Nicklaus solved it all for him. He picked up Jacko's marker. 'I don't think you would have missed it,' he told him. 'But I did not want to give you the opportunity. Ryder Cups should not be decided on such putts.'

champion. He qualified for the U.S. Open at 17, and a year later did so again, and played all four rounds. Walker Cup honors followed at Muirfield, Scotland, in 1959, and upon returning home, Nicklaus won the U.S. Amateur, repeating the triumph in 1961.

Years of Triumph

Clearly he had done all he could in amateur golf, and it was no surprise when he turned professional shortly afterwards. Great things were expected and duly delivered. His first tournament victory came the next year. It was not a bad one with which to start. No Southern Open or some such low-key tournament for Nicklaus. He just walked right in and claimed the Open. That triumph heralded a rivalry with

Arnold Palmer that would last the rest of the decade. But while Palmer's titles were collected over a relatively short period of time, Nicklaus just kept on winning.

The following year he won the Masters, the first of three triumphs in four years at Augusta. And so it went on. But it was in the twilight of his career that Nicklaus won the two titles of which perhaps he will retain the fondest memories. Twilight is, in this instance, a relative term. This being Nicklaus, his twilight began in 1979 and was still in full swing some seven years later.

He was first written off at the start of the 1980s. Going into that year's Open at Baltusrol, he had turned 40 and had not won for almost two years. He was no longer an overpowering force. But at least at Baltusrol, Nicklaus could recall fond memories. He had won one Open there already. And when he opened with a 63, a shiver went down the spine of the rest of the field. After two rounds the man closest to him was the Japanese Isao Aoki, and what happened thereafter was reminiscent of Nicklaus's contest against Watson at Turnberry. This time he was not to be denied.

A birdie at the 17th on the final day gave Nicklaus a two-stroke lead, and the reception he was given as he made his way up the final fairway left him in no doubt as to the affection in which he is held. The player who had been derided for being fat when he first appeared on the circuit was America's darling.

The Greatest Triumph?

He was even more so six years later when he won a record sixth Masters title in barely credible circumstances. This triumph came against a background of a playing career that was distinctly winding down. Nicklaus's considerable business interests, which include designing golf courses all over the world, were taking up more and more of his time. But the New World, fed up with hearing of constant European successes, craved one more Nicklaus offering and it came at his beloved Augusta.

Once more, he was the hero of a major championship that will be talked about for as long as the game is played. Again he showed that indomitable will to win. With 10 holes to play he was hardly a factor, particularly with the two dominant players of the day, Greg Norman and Seve Ballesteros, perched on top of the leader board.

He may be the fiercest competitor in golf but Jack also knows how to lose graciously as he proved during the '87 Ryder Cup (above).

Jack Nicklaus's golf has survived the ravages of time. Here we see him on his way to becoming the oldest winner of the Masters at 46 (below).

Nicklaus had begun the last day in contention, knowing he would need something like a 66 to retain an interest. That became a far-fetched proposition as he struggled over the opening holes. A bogey at the 6th, where he missed a short putt, appeared to sound the death knell.

But a birdie at the 9th was followed by another at the 10th and now Nicklaus was off on one of those charges on which he has a unique patent. The last 10 holes at Augusta he played in seven under par, and when Ballesteros found water at the 15th, and Norman bogied the last, Nicklaus was a winner once more. The photograph of him as he secured another birdie at the 17th, characterizes his gifts. His determination and sheer presence are written large across those soft features.

And so a week that had begun with Nicklaus cutting out a newspaper article that claimed he was finished had ended with the greatest triumph of the lot. The lesson was clear: with Nicklaus, the boundaries of possibility have had to be stretched further than ever before.

Right: The old alliance, Nicklaus and caddie Jimmy Dickinson pictured during the 1989 British Open at Troon.

GREG NORMAN

It is a curious fact that while golf historians would struggle to assess Greg Norman's worth as one of the great post-war players, the game's audience have no such problem. Few have ambivalent feelings towards Norman. You either think him God's gift to the game, or you consider his a talent squandered. Nothing illustrates the two sides' points of view more than the fact that while his supporters call him the Great White Shark, his detractors refer to him as the Great White Flag.

Certainly, Norman has supplied both sides with an inordinate amount of ammunition over the years. When Norman is good he is very special. Most of us have on instant recall the second round he played in the 1986 British Open at Turnberry. Remember the Ailsa course that year? Before the event

began there was a torrent of complaints as to the way it had been set up. In a knee-jerk reaction to the previous British Open at the venue in 1977, when even journeyman pros had gone around in 66, the fairways had been cut to a maximum 30 yards of width and, just to make things interesting, strong winds all week had added their contribution to protecting Turnberry's reputation. In that second round, many players struggled to break 80. Any would have been thrilled to shoot 70. Norman? He shot 63. He breezed to victory and no less a player than Tom Watson later referred to that 63 as 'the finest round in a tournament in which I have been a competitor.'

Yet it sums up the Norman enigma that a year that could have seen him immortalized by winning the Grand

Slam, ended with just that one major championship victory. It would have been excusable had one other major slipped from his grasp, two even. But to lose a winning position in all the other three confirmed to the 'white flag' lobby that here was a player who is one full stride short of greatness. Supplementing their argument is the fact he has also lost a play-off for the Open, and twice bogied the final hole to lose the Masters. On the other hand, his supporters point to the fact he is dogged by outrageous bad luck of a sort only previously suffered by, perhaps, Tony Jacklin.

Outrageous Fortune

Norman lost the 1986 PGA Championship when Bob Tway holed a bunker shot on the final hole. He lost the 1987 Masters when Larry Mize sank a 140ft chip shot over rolling terrain on the second hole of a sudden-death play-

Greg Norman about to lash a drive at Turnberry's picturesque 9th hole during his victorious final round in the 1986 British Open.

off. That was ill-luck, certainly. But it was Norman's mistakes over the closing holes that allowed his opponents to get into such a position. And so it was at the 1989 British Open at Royal Troon, where we were once more treated to Norman's imperious brand of golf over the opening holes when he started the final round with six straight birdies. From an also-ran position he even made the three-way play-off, and all the doubts seemed to have been cast aside as he began the four-hole affair with two straight birdies. But they resurfaced when, after a bogey four at the 17th (the third hole used), he indulged in a comedy of errors down the last, eventually putting his ball in his pocket and so conceding victory to Mark Calcavecchia.

Showdown at St. Andrews

In 1990, at St. Andrews, he was once more in contention, the joint leader after two rounds with Nick Faldo. But he was totally subdued in the third round, and even the fact he was leading the world rankings by a street at that point, can have been no consolation for another major slipping through his fingers.

Whatever the opinions about Norman, few can deny that he is good for the game. He began playing by chance, after caddying for his mother, a three-handicap player. Up to that point his muscular physique had been honed playing the sort of sports for which macho Australians are more typically renowned. Golf will be grateful that he was quick to see there was more to it than meets the eye. He adds undoubted panache to the Tour, and lucky indeed are the spectators who catch him when he is on the very top of his game.

He lives his life off the course at an equally breakneck pace. Friends like the British F1 racing driver Nigel Mansell indulge his love for the fast lane, and he once played in an Italian Open simply because he was already in Italy to supervise the purchase of a Ferrari Testarossa. Norman also tore down his $2 million home in Florida in order to build a $10 million one in its place. The message is that he is having fun. But he needs to claim a few more majors if he wants to join the game's immortals.

Greg Norman's victory at Turnberry will live with him forever. An anxious look is at odds with an eventual victory by five shots.

JOSÉ-MARIA OLAZÁBAL

Describing someone as being born to play golf is to imply that he had a natural empathy with the game from the start. In José-Maria Olazábal's case it is almost literally true. His mother Julia was still working on the yet to be opened San Sebastian course in the Spanish village of Fuenterrabia on the day before his birth. Thus the scent of the Royal and Ancient game was there with Olazábal when he first set eyes on the world. It has remained with him ever since.

Rising Star

Right from his amateur days, Olazábal looked to be the brightest prospect to emerge in European golf since the emergence of Faldo, Lyle and Ballesteros, and so it has thrillingly proved. He is a worthy successor to all of them, a man driven by victory to seek out still more of the same. Solitary as a child, it was not only because he lived on a golf course that he chose the game. It suited his personality exactly. Alongside a brilliant short game and accuracy with his woods and irons, Olazábal's greatest virtue is his intense concentration and ambition. There is no doubt that here is a young man destined for the game's very highest levels.

Nothing illustrated this more than his startling win in the World Series of Golf in 1990. An opening round of 61 on the fearsome Firestone course, a real contender for the round of the year, was followed by two 67s for an eight-shot lead with 18 holes to play. Did Olazábal rest on his laurels? Not likely. He went further away from the field, eventually winning by 12 shots, the biggest winning margin on the U.S. tour for 15 years.

He is prepared to make all the sacrifices necessary, although at one point he went too far and sacrificed his health. In 1988, on a rare opportunity to indulge his hobby of hunting in the mountains with his father, he felt giddy. A doctor later diagnosed an ulcer, a rare condition in a man of 23. He told Olazábal to worry all he liked on the course, but to forget it once the 18 holes were over.

Olazábal first made his name on the British amateur circuit. His visits were infrequent: what made them startling is that every time he came over he won. First it was the British Boys' Championship. Then the Amateur itself. When, in 1985, he collected the British Youths' Championship, he had completed a unique triumvirate of trophies, and with no amateur targets left to achieve, he headed off for fame and fortune on the pro circuits.

The Spanish Succession

The transition proved astonishingly straightforward. He was equally precocious at this much higher level. First Olazábal won the qualifying school, and then the following year finished runner-up in the European order of merit. He won two trophies, including one of the continent's great titles – the European Masters – and even the great Severiano Ballesteros, bowed his head in admiration. The following year they began what is already perhaps the most

The ball has long departed but José-Maria Olazábal's head is still down, peering at the spot which it left.

intense of all Ryder Cup partnerships. Ballesteros and Olazábal were sensational together in both 1987 and 1989 and lost only once in eight matches together. They exude an air of ferocious competitiveness. Their opponents recognize them as the most talented player in the world in tandem with the young master to whom he will bequeath the Spanish succession.

To watch them in action is mesmerizing, and while Ollie, as he is affectionately known, still knows his place — 'when Seve gets his Porsche going, not even San Pedro in heaven can stop him,' he said during the last match — he also feels no sense of awe. After all, he is (as Ballesteros insists) the best putter in the world from 10 feet. In-

deed, in the 1989 Ryder Cup, there were times when he scolded Ballesteros for what he saw as bad thinking, and he warned him on other occasions of the dangers that lay ahead. And it was Olazábal who emerged as the leading points winner at The Belfry, dropping only half a point in five matches.

In general, 1989 was a year when he enhanced a growing reputation. He finished second again in the money list, and in addition to winning twice, he racked up no less than 13 top-12 finishes elsewhere from just 19 events in total. It was a remarkable feat of consistency.

Olazábal can become one of the game's dominant forces in the 1990s.

José-Maria Olazábal was the star of the 1989 Ryder Cup, and he ended 1990 in third place in the world rankings.

There is little doubt that his appetite will remain. Olazábal has always insisted that he is in golf to win titles. He once said: 'It would make me a very sad man indeed if I left the game without having won at least one major championship.'

He started the 90s in fine style, winning the Benson & Hedges at St. Mellion, Cornwall, after a final-round head-to-head battle with the runner-up, Ian Woosnam. It was Ollie's first European Tour win in Britain — but assuredly not the last.

ARNOLD PALMER

Sometimes the bald facts of a man's career tell less than the full story. Arnold Palmer's is very much a case in point. History tells us his last major championship victory was 26 years ago; indeed, his days as a major winner lasted barely more than half a decade.

But Palmer's contribution to the Royal and Ancient game, as every student of the sport knows, extends far beyond mere winning. For Palmer showed the direction professional golf should take, and the path of those who followed in his footsteps has led us to the multi-billion dollar industry golf has become.

Palmer was a pioneer, the man who dragged golf into the second half of the 20th century. It is said he gave the game sex appeal and people loved the fact that, even when he owned his own jet, he insisted on returning to his hometown of Latrobe in Pennsylvania. To this day, Palmer has never forsaken his roots. What Palmer brought to golf

was the element of risk, the excitement of boldness. The five times Open champion Peter Thomson had epitomized the spirit of the game in the 50s with the comment that golf was all about judgement not power, and that its most important facets were careful planning, calm thinking and the ordinary logic of common sense.

It is a sound theory but it contains all the box-office appeal of a grass-growing festival. And it never appealed to Palmer. His father had taught him to hit the ball as far as he could and worry about direction later. When Palmer went on to the first tee, the *frisson* of excitement matched that felt when a boxer climbs through the ropes. Even today, what became known as 'Arnie's

---

The anoraks, the leggings, all signal a typical British summer's day but none of this bothered the masterly bad weather golfer Palmer on his way to his 1961 British Open win at Birkdale.

Army', is still a sizeable platoon. 'What other people might consider careless and foolish is my natural game,' he once said. 'It is my nature to hit a ball hard and usually go for everything and therefore it isn't reckless for me to do so.'

Raising an Army

The swashbuckling style quickly found an audience. Who would not warm to a man who, two up with three to play in the World Matchplay final, at Wentworth, England, took a driver off the 16th tee because 'to have taken a one-iron at that stage would have seemed chicken-hearted.' So much for judgement not power, and careful planning.

And for a while, Palmer's theories worked better than almost anyone's before or since. Between April 1958 and April 1964 he won seven of the 25 major championships held, an extraordinary success rate. No obstacle seemed too great. One shot behind Ken Venturi in the 1960 Masters with two holes to play? No problem. Palmer just birdied both holes. In the U.S. Open later that year, Palmer was seven strokes behind the leader Mike Souchak going into the final round, but once again no deficit seemed insurmountable as he produced a last round 65 to win.

Palmer was the ultimate gatecrasher, a man who would burst in just as someone else was preparing their victory speech. His appeal and his exploits brought golf to a wider audience and his patronage of the 1960 British Open was pivotal in breathing fresh life into what had become an ailing event.

Mind Game

Palmer is a great exemplar of the fact that golf is essentially a game played in the mind. When people gather to talk about the great swings there have been, Palmer would never be considered. When an American magazine once asked 25 professionals for their favourite swing, Palmer received just one vote – from Lee Trevino! But he compensated with the most indomitable will and with that came the ability to produce the most expert recovery shot when nothing else would do. Perhaps the prime example of this came in

1961 British Open at Royal Birkdale.

At the then 15th hole (now the 16th) on the final day, Palmer's errant tee shot came to rest at the base of a bush. All day he had been pursued by Dai Rees, and as the Welshman racked up birdies, Palmer knew he could not afford the sensible option of hitting a wedge back onto the fairway and accepting a five. An audible gasp went through the hushed galleries as he reached for a 5-iron. They realized he was going for the green which was fully 150 yards away. Palmer said afterwards he had never hit a ball so hard in his life. When he made contact with it, the bush separated its contact with the earth, and the ball hurtled towards the green, finishing 16 feet from the flag.

Above: Not all Arnold's shots finished in exactly the spots he intended. Here he peers intently at one that got away. Below: A throwback to the days when people went to golf tournaments to see one man.

Arnold Palmer in full flow, even at 60. This was his trademark, the high finish and the face flush with determination, and it was still there at the 1990 British Seniors Open at Turnberry.

Rees birdied three of the last four holes but lost by a stroke. The difference between the two is marked by a plaque on that hole.

Down to the Wire

Most of the other examples are to be found in his great feats of daring on the greens. It is no coincidence that two of Palmer's four Masters titles should have come from birdieing the final hole. It summed up the style of the man. The great Bobby Jones once said: 'He has the ability to stare the ball into the hole. If ever I had an 8ft putt and everything depended on it, I would want Arnold Palmer to putt it for me.'

If Palmer had a weakness during those years it was his wedge play, a failing he shared with Jack Nicklaus. But that does not explain how a player could win so often in such a short space of time and then never win another major championship. In the years since 1964 Palmer was in contention to win a major championship on only about six occasions. It was a marked decline in his playing influence and it cannot be put down to age. He was just 34 when he tasted his last success. Perhaps the old cliché of he who lives by the sword also perishes by it provides a sounder base.

Certainly, part of Palmer's problems can be traced to the waning of his extraordinary powers on the world's putting surfaces. No longer did the putts go in as of right, and as they stopped so Palmer no longer could afford — and perhaps no longer had the nerve — to be quite so aggressive. (It is an experience Tom Watson has also had to come to terms with.)

But all that is irrelevant now. Let us glory in the legend. Palmer's place in the pantheon is assured. He has given the greater portion of his adult life to his sport, and if he was rewarded with riches then unparalleled in the game, surely that is what pioneers deserve.

Arnold Palmer plays out of one of Troon's deep bunkers. Eleven years before, and on the same course, he had won the British Open for the second successive year.

GARY PLAYER

Player looks at life through eyes saturated in optimism. Don't ever mention the word 'can't' in his company – well, not unless you want a half-hour lecture on the subject. 'The word "can't" does not exist in my vocabulary,' was how he opened an instruction book. Its title was Golf Begins at Fifty. We should have expected nothing else from a man who had just passed that landmark.

Whereas even the greatest players like Jack Nicklaus talk about the inevitable progress of *anno domini*, Player still refuses to recognize it. At the first major championship of this decade, the Masters, he still believed, at the age of 54, that he could win. Player is an original, a man driven like no other to get the very best out of what nature gave him. Truly, when he eventually slows down and sits in an armchair to con-

template his life, he can say with hand on heart, that he did everything possible to fuel his ambition to be remembered as the greatest golfer who ever lived. He realized from an early age that to get the most from a small and relatively puny frame, he would have to subject himself to the most arduous fitness regime ever undertaken by any golfer.

Practice Makes Perfect

Player is still at it now. He conditioned himself by running miles daily to im-

Gary Player wearing his familiar black clothing and a determined expression.

prove his leg strength and stamina, and then would finish off with 70 or 80 fingertip push-ups each day to build up his hands, arms, and back. After that, he would practice like few others before or since. Ben Hogan, a man who matched him in this respect, and who hands out compliments like they were $10,000 bills, once said: 'I know how hard Player has worked. He is doing what I advocated, and that is working hard on fundamentals, and then working the fundamentals into his game.'

One priceless story exemplifies Player's indomitable dedication to better himself. As a teenager he would practice his bunker shots at the Virginia Park course in Johannesburg. It was six o'clock in the morning. At 12 noon, the club professional happened to pass by the same bunker. There was Player still blasting away. A clue perhaps as to why he is recognised as one of the finest exponents of sand shots that the game has known. Given this background of hard work, concentration, and attention to detail, it is not surprising that Player should have remained at the top of his profession for as long as he did.

He won nine major championships in all, the first in 1959, the last almost 20 years later in 1978 and is only the fourth man in history to have won all four of the majors at least once.

Victories on the Road

What lends particular weight to Player's achievements of course, is that every major he won was in an alien environment, away from his beloved homeland. Whereas most of the great players have been American, thereby competing in three major championships each year on home soil, Player has always had to travel thousands of miles. Then again, that just goes with the territory for someone with Player's outlook on life.

His first overseas expedition was in 1955 to England. He prepared for it by practising in downpours to get used to the conditions he was expecting. Even so, his hosts were not impressed: he had the most appalling 'hooker's' grip. But Player has never been stubborn in his approach to golf. The next time he came, after noting Dai Rees's weaker grip, he had a 'slicer's' hold on the club. Clearly something somewhere in the middle was called for and when Player found it, the trophies he craved followed quickly.

On his next British visit he won the Dunlop tournament at Sunningdale, and thoughts quickly turned to the U.S. Tour. There the fitness-and-prac-

tice regime was taken to new heights. Player started wearing black because he believed it absorbed the sun's rays.

He won his first major at the 1959 British Open at Muirfield, and then turned his attention to the Masters. One noted professional of the day thought he could never win at Augusta because he was not long enough off the tee. Neither was Player but, of course, he did not understand the meaning of the word never. He consulted a body builder to see how he could add strength. He collected his first Masters title in 1961. Player would win three in all. And by 1965, when still not 30, he had won each of the majors once. It was

No-one ever concentrated harder or applied themselves more than Gary Player. Look at this for a perfect example of keeping your head down.

one of his finest years.

He won his only U.S. Open title that year, and then came an unforgettable triumph in the then Piccadilly World Matchplay Championship at Wentworth, England. In the semi-finals he was six down at lunch to Tony Lema and people were talking of a defeat of humiliating proportions. All except Player of course. He was not even thinking about making the loss margin respectable. He still believed he could

Player's mastery of the bunker shot is widely acknowledged by his fellow pros.

win and over the course of an extraordinary afternoon he did just that, squaring the match on the 36th, before claiming victory on the first extra hole.

Person-to-person combat was made for someone with Player's will to win and his record of five Matchplay victories still stands. By this time, he was one of the so-called 'big three,' the only time anyone ever referred to Player as big.

The other two were Arnold Palmer and Jack Nicklaus and over the first six years of the 1960s, they took the game to new heights.

Player and the Golden Bear continued to have a major say in how the game was played for many years. In 1974, for example, the former won both the Masters and the British Open titles. 'Gary just likes beating people,' was how one professional summed him up, and that philosophy continues as Player racks up more successes on the Seniors' Tour. On becoming eligible, he won four of his first eight

events. Ask Player why he is still so successful and he will put it down to God and the virtues of clean living. He says he has seen victories before they have actually happened. At the 1965 U.S. Open, just before the start of the final round, he tells the story of how he walked past a board detailing the names of former winners, and saw, in gold lettering, the words: '1965 – Gary Player.' Twenty-four hours later, it came to pass. The cynical furrow their brows at this and say he is too good to be true. But there are times in life when you can be just too cynical.

RONAN RAFFERTY

If Ronan Rafferty goes on to become one of the game's dominant forces in the 90s, students of the sport will pinpoint the fall of 1989 as the moment when the Northern Irishman truly showed he was blessed with the right stuff. From the pit of adversity Rafferty emerged to dominate the best players in Europe and America over a glorious six-week spell.

For years, Rafferty had looked likely to break through and join the European élite. Now, on the second day of the Ryder Cup, it seemed as if those ambitions were fatally flawed. Rafferty was playing with Christy O'Connor, Jnr., in a foursomes match against Mark Calcavecchia and Ken Green, and he could do little right. The home pair lost 3&2 and Rafferty came off the course de-vastated. On top of all that, he learned that his crucial singles match the next day would be against one of the men who had just beaten him mercilessly, Calcavecchia, the British Open champion.

It was in that singles match that Rafferty discovered the inner strength to support his belief that he could compete with the best. He came to the last hole all-square with his illustrious opponent. And there it was Calcavecchia's nerve that cracked. It was he who drove into the water, and it was Rafferty who emerged with a vital point.

The following week he defeated U.S. Open champion Curtis Strange in the Dunhill Cup. Then there was a win over Sandy Lyle in the Suntory World Matchplay, before his most important victory yet, in the Volvo Masters, after a thrilling head-to-head duel with Nick Faldo. In six weeks, Rafferty had defeated no less than four of the winners of the previous eight major championships. He ended the year with three titles to his name and on top of the European money list, with over $700,000 earned.

The seeds of a brilliant amateur career, when he became the youngest player ever to compete in the Walker Cup, had truly burst into bloom.

The day Ronan Rafferty came of age. The 18th hole at Valderrama and he realizes that he has won the Volvo Masters, after a thrilling head-to-head duel with Nick Faldo.

PAYNE STEWART

It is easy to get the wrong idea about William Payne Stewart. People look at his garish (if color-coordinated) clothing and assume he has something to hide. Whatever that may be, its certainly not lack of talent.

He also gave abundant evidence that he is a true sportsman on two notable occasions in 1989. The first came in the PGA Championship when Stewart finally ended years of disappointment to win his first major. It was his finest moment, but he went out of his way to offer consoling words to Mike Reid, the runner-up, who had thrown away the lead (as he had also done in the Masters a few months before). Stewart said: 'I can't help but feel for Mike. I too have messed up a few tournaments in my time. I know exactly what he is going through.' And, like Kipling's exemplar, he showed he could handle disaster as well as triumph a month later at the Ryder Cup. This time he had to swallow the bitterest of pills. He was one up in his singles match against José-Maria Olazábal, just as he had been the previous day in a four-ball game while partnering Curtis Strange. On that occasion, they had lost both the final two holes to Mark

James and Howard Clark and fell to unexpected defeat. Now, against Olazábal, he was one of three Americans hypnotized by the water on the 18th hole. But instead of running off and sulking in a corner, Stewart put his arm around his young opponent and congratulated him not only on that triumph but on the way he had performed all week.

Stewart's golf career began and progressed in orderly fashion through junior and high school programmes before he earned a golf scholarship to Southern Methodist University. While there he won several collegiate events. Although he failed at his first attempt at the U.S. Tour qualifying school, he prepared for his future career by playing two years in Asia. When he returned, maturity had set in and he won a tournament in his very first year on tour. He won another the following season as well and now he was being talked of in terms of the best of the post-Watson generation.

Wheel of Fortune

It did not work out that way. Stewart lost the winning habit. Four years he

endured without another victory, although he kept the dollar wheels turning nicely in his bank account, by usually finishing in the top 10. Indeed, so often was Stewart runner-up, he earned the nickname 'Avis,' after the company that always finishes second in the car hire market.

At least he kept the frustration he was feeling in perspective. When he did finally break the sequence, in the 1987 Hertz Bay Hill Classic, 'Avis' donated the entire six figure first prize to a Florida hospital in memory of his father, who had died two years previously to the day. In between, major championship scars had also accumulated. He finished second in the 1985 British Open at Sandwich. And in the 1986 U.S. Open, he led by three shots with six holes to play, only to crumble under the intimidating eye of Raymond Floyd. He was defiant in defeat. 'Raymond has not seen the Taj Mahal, the Great Wall of China — or the last of me,' he said.

In 1989, he was proved right. He began the year by saying: 'I don't care if people do not believe I can win tournaments. All that matters is I know I can,' and he was right about that too. First he won the Heritage Classic in Kiawah Island in April. And then came that first major championship victory, when he had five birdies in his last seven holes to catch Reid at the last gasp. It was a win that clinched for him a place in the U.S. Ryder Cup side that was captained by Ray Floyd.

Stewart is easily identifiable by his wearing of plus-fours that earn him $600,000 a year courtesy of the National Football League. In return he wears the NFL colors of the team in whatever town the tour happens to be appearing that week. But next time you pass judgement, look beyond the outlandish clothing. Inside it there is a true sportsman, not to mention a very good golfer, eagerly looking out.

Left: Stylish in dress, stylish in swing. Few players are more accurate off the tee than Payne Stewart. However, his accuracy crucially deserted him on the final hole in the 1989 Ryder Cup (right) where a drive into the water cost him his match with Olazábal.

CURTIS STRANGE

When Curtis Strange successfully defended his U.S. Open title in 1989, he proved to a suspicious world what America had known for some time: here was a player that deserved to be ranked alongside the very best of today's élite performers; a man who had been tested in the crucible of competition and emerged with the toughest of protective shields. These days Strange is recognized as the most redoubtable of performers, a man who revels in those situations when heart and pulse are hammering.

It was not always this way. Indeed, Strange was tipped for stardom after playing in the 1975 Walker Cup but admitted later he could not handle the pressure of the qualifying school and hopelessly missed the cut. He was taught the fundamentals of the game by his father, who was the professional and owner of the White Sands Country Club in Virginia. He encouraged his son's insatiable appetite for practice that is still prevalent in Strange today. But his father died of lung cancer while Strange was still a teenager, and the memory – whenever it is raised at press conferences – still causes him to wince. He vowed there and then to win a major championship and dedicate it to his father's memory.

Fuelled by his loss, Strange gave up a promising talent as a baseball pitcher and imposed an even stricter regime of practice upon himself. At times he tried too hard. When he qualified to go on to the U.S. tour, he quickly fell out with his fellow professionals who were upset at his constant complaining. Strange was one of those characters who would whine because he hit the left hand side of the fairway when he was aiming for the right. And when he missed it altogether he would launch into a cascade of swearing. In Britain, his reputation was no better. He came across as the shallowest of characters, with dollar signs in his eyes: he decided to miss the British Open one year, and then came over the following week for the Dutch Open upon receipt of the requisite amount of appearance money.

Growing into the Job

Over the years, however, Strange has matured without ever losing that raw competitive hunger. One turning point came in Arnold Palmer's tournament, the Bay Hill Classic. Strange had gone to university on an Arnold Palmer sports scholarship and had become interested in the game in the first place

Strange drives across the Swilcan Burn during his 1988 Dunhill match against Ireland's D'Arcy.

after watching the great man on television. One can imagine the shame and the humiliation, when, after hearing that he had lost his temper on the course, Palmer gave Strange a public dressing down.

After that Strange kept himself under a tight reign, and his maturity was evident in the 1985 Masters at Augusta. There he was set to complete the finest comeback in the history of the event. He had begun it as one of the favorites but a first round 80 saw him bringing up the rear. Strange followed it with a

A bad moment but Curtis Strange still went on to win the 1988 US Open at Brookline beating Faldo in the play-off.

65 to make the halfway cut and then 68 to move into the top ten.

With six holes to go he hit the front and comparison could be made with a 1500-meter runner who slips on the first bend, only to make up for the error when the tape comes into view. But there was no sprint finish from Strange. At the 13th he put his second shot into Rae's Creek that fronts the green. At the 15th he compounded the felony and again found water. The title went to Bernhard Langer. But on the course there were no expressions of anger. And far from missing a post-event press conference, or giving excuses, Strange opened his heart and gave the most moving account of what he had been through. And he never forgot the wise advice of Jack Nicklaus who told him the experience would either make him as a golfer or scar him for life.

The Will to Win

In Strange's case, it certainly was the former. His nerve to win his first major, the 1988 U.S. Open at Brookline was cast-iron, as he defeated Nick Faldo in an 18 hole play-off. Afterwards, his was again the press conference to attend as he spoke eloquently about having kept his unspoken promise to his father to win a major. And having taken 33 years to reach the winner's circle, Strange showed his extreme reluctance to leave it the following year, when he was again in the right place to pick up the pieces when Tom Kite folded on the final day.

Strange then capped a memorable year in the Ryder Cup with the sort of finish in the final match which only enhanced his tough-guy reputation. The position was this: he was involved in the final game out on the course, America was trailing by one point overall and Strange, with four holes to play, was one down himself. He therefore had to win at least two of the last four holes against, of all competitors, the tough little Welshman Ian Woosnam, if his country was not to suffer the indignity of a third straight Ryder Cup loss.

Many players would have died inwardly there and then, but as is probably obvious by now, Strange more than likely grew a couple of inches at the prospect. His response was to birdie each of the next three holes, and from one down he was one up going to the last tee. Still he was not safe. The final hole at The Belfry is laden with disaster. Paul Azinger, Payne Stewart and Mark Calcavecchia had all driven into the water on that very day. Severiano Ballesteros had hit his second shot into another water hazard. Strange played the hole in a way that brooked no argument. He never let Woosnam's hopes rise for a second. His tee shot dissected the fairway. And then his 3-iron approach never left the flag's direction for any of its 210 yards. It bounced once, 20ft short of the pin, before nestling 4 feet away. Strange had saved American honor. By this time of course, we had come to expect nothing less.

Feeling much better! Strange on his way to retaining the US Open title in 1989 having clinched yet another birdie at the 16th.

LEE TREVINO

Before American tournament golf recruitment became one long procession from the collegiate ranks, it was a profession peopled by men from all walks of life. The school most of them had known was the one that delivered hard knocks for lessons. Of this dying breed, Lee Trevino was, until he joined the Seniors in 1990, one of the few to have survived. Against a background of players who look as if they were cast from the same mold, Trevino stands out like the proverbial sore thumb. Once a marine, twice-married, three times he has made a fortune and lost it. Today he is rich once more, con-

tented, and safely enshrined as one of the game's legends.

Out of the Unknown

When Trevino came out of the marines in the early 60s, he was already a very good player. He had learned his skills in quite outrageous fashion with hustled bets on a par-three course in Dallas. Using an old fruit-juice bottle swathed in tape to prevent it shattering, he would take on all-comers using that as a club, while others could use conventional weapons. Trevino would display his exceptional hand-eye co-ordination. He

would throw the ball in the air, and hit it baseball-style. On the greens he used the bottle like a snooker cue for putting. He once went around a full nine holes in just 29 strokes!

And he practised like the devil. He says his normal daily regime was 18 holes of golf in the morning then some 1,000 balls on the practice range for the rest of the day and evening. There he 'grooved' that somewhat ungainly swing – a swing that seems to blow a calculated raspberry at every coaching manual ever written. Trevino has a slicer's stance, and at the top of the backswing, the clubface is closed, like a hooker's. But everything comes right at the point of impact. The American professional George Archer once summed

It doesn't look too promising but Trevino went on to birdie the hole and then win the tournament at the 1971 British Open.

The U.S. PGA championship fell to Trevino in 1984 after four rounds in the 60s.

always go down well with his fellow professionals and Jacklin once told him he was not going to talk during a round. As ever, Trevino had an answer. 'Don't talk,' he said. 'Just listen.' Supermex continued on his merry way.

He won the PGA Championship in 1974, making it five majors in just six years. But luck finally ran out the following year when he was struck by lightning during the final round of the Western Open. Trevino has been reminded of his own mortality ever since because he has been plagued from that moment on by back problems, and at various times has had to undergo surgery.

Who knows how many more major championships he would have won had he not had to severely cut down on that punishing practice schedule that had proved so successful? As it is, his only major victory after that date was one soaked in emotion, the 1984 PGA, when his closest pursuer was one of his longest rivals, Gary Player.

The Missing Piece

The Masters is the one piece missing from a Trevino 'grand slam' of the major championships. At this event, there is the only visible sign of the boy who grew up with a chip on his shoulder. When Trevino was as good as anybody, he deeply resented the Masters system of a locker room for former winners, and another locker room for everybody else. To this day he refuses to recognize what he sees as a two-tier class system. Trevino has always changed his shoes in the parking lot at Augusta.

It is the action of a man who, for all that smiling exterior and attractive personality, remains an enigma. After the completion of a round, you won't see him having a beer with his professional friends and laughing and joking. You rarely see him in a restaurant. For Trevino, public life ends the moment he leaves the golf course, at which point he puts on the most private of hats. The costume change comes easily to him, after all these years.

These days, his adoring audience is more likely to find him on the Seniors' tour, or with the 'fat-bellies' as he calls them. Trevino does not need to play this circuit for money, but he does so because, like Player, he will never lose the thrill of competition. Here is a tour where he is likely to be first among equals for a good while yet.

up the Trevino swing. He said in 1973: 'The swing that repeats most often on tour today is Lee Trevino's. I have seen him score badly when he is thinking badly but I have never seen him swing badly. That little old swing just keeps repeating, and repeating and...'

At that time Trevino was arguably the best golfer in the world, but six years earlier he was totally unknown. He rose to national prominence in the most mercurial manner, after his first wife Claudia cashed in her savings to enter her husband in the 1967 Open at Baltusrol. Trevino finished fifth. Sometimes such performances are never repeated but the cheerful Mexican swiftly dissuaded anyone with a mind to think that way by winning the event the following year at Oak Hill.

Don't Talk – Just Listen

By now he was developing a public persona that we all have come to know so well. He would chat all the time to the galleries, even when about to take his address position. His audience in turn loved his relaxed manner, a refreshing departure from a largely colorless professional scene.

The U.S. Open is not really Trevino's event since it almost invariably favors those who hit the ball high, but he showed there is no legislating for genius by winning the event again three years later (1971) at Merion.

Then he turned his attention to the British Open, which suited his extravagant range of shots perfectly. Trevino quickly fell in love with the British game, and, as U.S. Open Champion, won at Royal Birkdale in 1971. He tested the loyalty of his audience severely the next year, however, by riding some outrageous luck to defeat the home favorite Tony Jacklin and successfully defend the title. On show here were the magical powers he had displayed to the Dallas hustlers, but in between there were some strokes that belonged only to sorcery. Like holing a bunker shot on the 'fly.'

Trevino's constant chatter did not

Above: A typically ebullient Trevino plays to the gallery during the 1985 British Open. Left: It's much easier on the senior's tour! Trevino reaches the end of a hot afternoon's work at the 1989 British Open.

TOM WATSON

If truly great players earn that title because of the aura of invincibility they take onto a golf course, then Tom Watson can be said to rank among the very best. For eight long years, Watson walked onto the first tee of the world's most important golf championships and all the talk was of who would claim second place. During that time – a time when Jack Nicklaus, Lee Trevino and Raymond Floyd were all powerful forces, and Nick Faldo, Sandy Lyle, and Severiano Ballesteros emerging ones – none could hold a candle to Watson who walked off with the British Open on no less than five occasions.

Teenage Sensation

While the record books state that the great Harry Vardon won the British Open more times than Watson, many believe the American to be the greatest links player of them all. Born in Kansas – far from any seaside golf course – Watson did have a few balls bouncing in his favor. One was a scratch golfer for a father, who introduced his son to the game at an early age. There is a lovely story of the time that Watson senior was asked to leave a course as his seven-year-old son was considered too young to play. Watson countered by asking whether, if Tom cleared a brook 75 yards off the first tee with his cutdown 3-wood, that would be considered a valid signature of his ability? The professional agreed. With family honour at stake, Tom proceeded to clear the brook with many yards to spare. Another seven years and the scratch golfer found he could no longer defeat his talented son. At 13 Watson had won the Kansas City matchplay tournament and at 15 played an 18-hole contest for charity against no less a figure than Arnold Palmer. Nerves? What nerves? On the first tee, Watson hit his drive 300 yards. 'Who's this?' Arnold is said to have exclaimed. He was to find out soon enough.

Left: Watson squints into the late afternoon sun during the 1988 U.S. PGA at Oak Tree.

Right: Long off the tee – even as a fifteen year-old Watson had astounded Arnold Palmer by hitting a 300-yard drive at the first hole of a charity game.

Tom Watson won the British Open five times in the late seventies and early eighties but Harry Vardon's record of six remains.

But if Watson displayed the coolest of temperaments as an amateur, things were different as he strove to establish himself on the U.S. Tour. Laughable as it seems now, Watson was branded a 'choker' by certain sections of the media after losing strong positions in both the 1974 and 1975 U.S. Opens and the 1975 Masters. Such talk did not last very long. The British Open, July 1975, the venue Carnoustie, saw the start of the Watson British Open dynasty. A birdie on the final hole gave him an 18-hole play-off with the Australian Jack Newton, and the next day Watson shot 71, Newton 72, and that elusive first major championship victory was his.

Victory Procession

After that, Watson could not stop winning majors. He collected the first of his two Masters victories in 1977, but the victory that was the spur towards immortality came in a never-to-be-forgotten British Open that year at Turnberry. It will go down as the greatest British Open of them all, and how appropriate Watson should win it, a man who had grown to respect and love links golf. Each British Open, he would come over a couple of weeks early simply to play the best seaside courses the British Isles can offer. The admiration was mutual. On this occasion Watson even defeated the most favored son of all, Jack Nicklaus. It was golf of a quality rarely seen before as the two best players of the day pushed each other to new heights. Watson shot 65, 65. Nicklaus 65, 66. The rest of the field seemed to be playing in a different tournament. And on that final day, Watson showed another attribute the great ones possess: the ability to conjure the most precise shot at exactly the right moment. On this occasion it came at the short 15th. Watson was trailing by one shot, and had pulled his tee shot. Nicklaus was safely on the green, and in a position, to extend his advantage. Watson then proceeded to hole the most astonishing of putts from all of 20 yards. And after Nicklaus had dropped a shot at the 17th, Watson made sure of victory with a majestic 7-iron approach to the home hole that finished a mere two feet from the flag.

If Nicklaus supporters felt aggrieved, Watson, five years later, proved it was no fluke by claiming the U.S. Open in almost identical circumstances. Again these two were the leading protagonists. The venue was one of the supreme courses in America, Pebble Beach in California, and the drama of the occasion was heightened because this was a major title Watson had still to claim despite the fact that by this time he had won six others.

Repeat Performance

With two holes to play, Nicklaus had set the target in the clubhouse, with Watson level with him standing on the 17th tee. A treacherous short hole, the title seemed Nicklaus's when Watson hooked his 2-iron shot. The ball nestled in deep rough and just to complete the picture, the flag had been cut close to the spot in which his ball was lying. To get down in two from a position where the ball was bound to 'fly,' on the lightning fast green, appeared to be asking too much even of the man with the magical short game. But Watson did not earn that reputation for nothing. He cut a sand wedge, the ball landed on the edge of the green, picked up pace, and dropped into the hole. It was a shot as memorable as any played in the 80s and it secured for him the title he had begun to think he would not win.

Record Under Threat

By now that aura of invincibility was so strong that a month later, an intimidated Nick Price handed him the British Open at Troon. A year later Watson successfully defended it, winning his fifth in nine years at Royal Birkdale. He had won five major championships in four years and now even Nicklaus's record of 18, which everyone had automatically assumed would stand for eternity, appeared under threat.

Beginning of the End

How ironic, then, that the very tournament that marked the zenith of his powers should, in 1984, bring him to his knees. This time, Watson was going for a hat-trick of British Open wins at St. Andrews, the one Scottish venue where he had still to claim the glittering prize. With two holes to play he was in position to set the record straight and tie Vardon's record. He was tied for first place with the best the developing European game could offer, Seve Ballesteros. Watson had hit the perfect drive down the notorious Road Hole, but was plagued by indecision over his second shot. He was torn between a 2- and 3-iron, and perhaps reminded of the magnificent rapier thrust he had struck into the heart of the final green a year earlier with the same club, he selected the former. It proved his undoing. The ball flew over the green, and on to the road behind. Watson registered a bogey at precisely the moment Ballesteros, a hole ahead, picked up a birdie. The British Open was over for Watson and gone with it was that aura.

Powers in Decline

For the rest of the decade he was never the same man. His finest quality, alongside an innate competitive streak, had always been his bold putting stroke. How much easier putting is when you can trundle the ball 3ft past with the first effort, absolutely convinced you would hole the return. But Watson started missing the returns, and so it followed his first putts were no longer struck with the same confidence. Financially secure, he found his interest in the game waning.

The decade ended with Watson in a rather healthier state. He was a factor in both the 1989 British Open and U.S.PGA events and while he won neither the fact that he was back in contention helped his confidence sufficiently to play a leading role in the 1989 tied Ryder Cup match. At 41, he had done enough to convince us that we should wait a while yet before drawing a line under his record of eight major championships.

A superbly accurate and bold putter Watson's game went into decline as his putting confidence diminished.

IAN WOOSNAM

There is no ideal height, weight or build for a professional golfer but whenever a composite picture is produced, for the sake of hypothesis, Ian Woosnam is always the antithesis of it. It is just one of the many ways in which he has overcome adversity to establish himself among the finest players of his generation.

Woosnam stands just 5ft 4in tall and for no less than five years was faced with overwhelming evidence that his ambition of becoming a top tournament professional was a waste of time.

Woosie, as he is popularly known, scraped a living by the most tortured of means. He travelled round in a battered van. Nothing in his record sug-

gested he could become the player of his dreams. Even as an amateur he had no record to speak of. All he really had was his own desire — but sometimes that is enough.

Toughing it Out

The pugnacity that saw him hand out a bloody nose to anyone who picked on him because of his size at school carried him through the hard times. For

---

Woosnam occasionally has his putting problems but is the envy of many with his rhythmic and superbly simple swing.

each of those struggling years Woosnam went to the European Tour's qualifying school, only to fail to secure his card. It was a timely piece of advice from Gordon J Brand that turned his whole career around. The Englishman brought home to him the point that others had tried to make with little success, namely that he was too hard on himself. Woosnam watched Brand win a Safari tournament and marvelled at the way he refused to let the unluckiest of bounces or the poorest of shots ruffle him.

That year Woosnam finished third on the Safari Tour and now he was exempt from qualifying. Free from worrying about the next meal ticket, he made the breakthrough, winning the Swiss Open. Two years later he won the Scandinavian Open, and in 1985 he finished 4th in the European order of merit, and played a modest part in the recovery of the Ryder Cup at The Belfry.

If Woosnam had arrived in most people's eyes he had still to fulfil his own expectations. He believed, arrogantly perhaps, that he had a long game the equal of anyone in the world, but on the greens he was no better than average. It meant that he was still some way short of the status attained by his old sparring partner Sandy Lyle. But Woosnam found the elixir on the greens upon his return to The Belfry in the fall of 1986. There he won the Lawrence Batley International. The feeling was that once Woosnam started winning again he would not know how to stop.

Into the Rankings

So it proved in 1987 when he had a record better than any other player in the world. Woosnam won on no less than seven occasions, on three different continents — a world class player in the true sense of the word. The victory roll began in Hong Kong, continued in Europe, and concluded in America, where he led Wales to its finest hour and victory in the World Cup. Woosnam won the individual honors by the length of one of his drives, and he would be a key member of another victorious European Ryder Cup side. At Muirfield Village, Ohio, he teamed up with Nick Faldo in one of the great partnerships in the history of the competition. They have now played eight times together, and have lost just once.

Disappointingly for Woosnam, the decade ended with him still awaiting the major championship victory his ability undoubtedly deserves. In 1989 he tip-toed to the brink of winning in

Ian Woosnam, pictured in the Welsh hill country, seems to have found a difficult lie.

his first U.S. Open. In any event it was an astonishing performance to claim a tie for runners-up spot, and it needed some commanding golf down the final holes from the defending champion Curtis Strange to deny him. Similarly in the PGA Championship there was another top five finish.

Most golf crowds love him, and marvel at his inordinate length from such a compact form. The key rests on a God-given sense of timing, plus forearms that would do justice to Popeye. Woosnam developed those on the farm his father owns near the Shropshire town of Oswestry, on the borders of England and Wales, where Ian still lives.

FUZZY ZOELLER

Fuzzy Zoeller will be remembered for his colorful personality, his humor, and his major championship victories – and in particular, for one golden moment when he pulled all those strands together. The occasion was the 1984 U.S. Open at Winged Foot, when Zoeller was in a race for the title with Greg Norman.

The Australian was playing in the group ahead of him on the final day and when he holed a 30ft putt on the final green, Zoeller took in the whoopin' and the hollerin' and thought it was all over: he thought Norman had secured a birdie and with it victory, but instead of pressing his chin against his chest and cursing his luck, Zoeller beamed a broad smile, and took the towel from his bag. It was white and he held it up in a mock act of sur-

A memorable career but how much more would Fuzzy Zoeller (below) have achieved if he had not been plagued by back problems? Here the effort of crouching down to read a putt is all too much.

render. It was a supreme act of sportsmanship. And, as subsequent events were to prove, unnecessary. Norman's putt, in fact, was for a par, and so the pair finished tied after 72 holes. The next day, it was no contest. Zoeller shot 67, Norman 75.

Debutant Winner

Zoeller had added the U.S. Open to the Masters title he had won in similarly sensational style five years earlier. It was his first appearance at Augusta, but he showed the same devil-may-care attitude that has been a hallmark of his career. Once more after 72 holes he had tied someone else, in this case Tom Watson and Ed Sneed, for the winning score. Once more Zoeller won the play-off, though this time it was the sudden-death version. He triumphed at the second extra hole. Not since Horton Smith won the first Masters in 1934 and Gene Sarazen in 1935 had a debutant won this title.

Zoeller's nickname comes from his

initials. He was baptized Frank Urban Zoeller, but somehow Fuzzy is much more appropriate, an illustration of his fun approach to life. He hails from Indiana and like every Hoosier, his first love was basketball. Ultimately it would be his fondness for that game that would hinder his progress in his second love, golf. For it was in high school basketball that he picked up the back problems that have never left him. Zoeller's method of address and swing only exacerbate the problem. He stands crouched low over the ball, and from the top of the backswing unleashes a whiplash action that puts untold pressure on his lower back.

For years, while Zoeller was entertaining the crowd with his non-stop chatter à la Trevino, he would be hurting on the inside. And it was after that triumph in the 1984 Open that he gave into the pain and underwent back surgery. The extent of the problem became public the week of that year's PGA Championship. As U.S. Open champion, Zoeller was clearly in the news and people were asking him if he could win two majors in the same year. Zoeller was wondering if he would be able to make it to the first tee.

The answer was no. On the morning of the first round, he could not move and he was rushed to hospital, where he remained for a week. At the end of the season, he went to the Hospital for Special Surgery in New York where he underwent an operation for two ruptured discs. Such was the seriousness of that operation, there were fears that he would never play again. Thankfully, they proved unfounded. But they have curtailed his chances of improving still further on a worthy record. He has not really been the same player since. He won no less than three tournaments in 1986, illustrating that he had not lost the knack for making the victory circle. But he had to cut down on his schedule and his practice routine, and in the end those wins are poignant reminders of what might have been but for an unfortunate accident in High School.

Right: Fuzzy blasts out of a bunker during the 1983 Masters. Three years previously he had won the tournament with superbly consistent scoring.

THE COURSES

AUGUSTA

Augusta National was the dream of Bobby Jones. Since the day it was created it has been the dream of everyone else who ever picked up a golf club to visit it. Television fleshes out the legend, the immaculate fairways, the breathtaking bunkers, the imperious greens. The wonder of it all is that the visitor does not feel a sense of anti-climax.

Bob Torrance, the noted coach and once a golf course manager, came away enthralled by his first visit. 'I have walked around every inch during these last three days, and have still to see so much as one weed!' he exclaimed. It is, indeed, the condition of Augusta that first overwhelms. Jones envisaged the course as open only to winter play, and Augusta still closes down after each Masters tournament in April. Thus does the turf retain its spring and its vigor. Even in the winter it is hardly overplayed. Membership is small and exclusive, being limited mainly to plutocrats or the politically eminent. One of the snow white houses that lines the 10th belonged to that well-known golf fanatic-turned-President, Dwight D Eisenhower.

The dream of Bobby Jones (above) was fleshed out by Alister Mackenzie whose subtle craft gave the 13th green (below) a deceptively tranquil appearance. The reality is Rae's Creek, which penalizes many an ill-judged shot.

Jones, the greatest amateur golfer of all time, retired in 1930 having won all there was to win; that year, indeed, he had won the British Open and U.S. Open titles, plus the British and U.S. Amateur Championships. Jones had won on courses as great as Merion, St. Andrews, Winged Foot and Oakmont, and now he wanted to create a course that reflected all their best attributes. It was to be a playground where he could invite his friends – amateurs and professionals – from all over the world to play golf. And when he set eyes on an old nursery called Fruitlands outside Augusta, Georgia, he knew he had found his piece of heaven. It had been owned by a Belgian horticulturist named Baron Berckmann, and so already in place were many of the stunningly colorful flora that delight us all each April.

Masterpiece in the Making

Jones could hardly believe his luck. It had the gentle hills as well that would capture the spirit of the British links courses which he loved so much. Together with his friend, a well-to-do New Yorker called Clifford Roberts, they

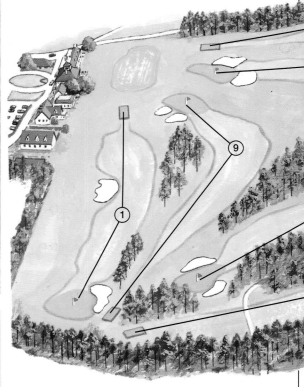

bought all 625 acres at depression prices. Although Jones had definite ideas on what sort of golf course he wanted, he was not a vain man. With his record he could have gone ahead and designed in any style he liked and people would have accepted it. But Jones wanted a masterpiece that would last for eternity and he had no hesitation in calling in Dr. Alister Mackenzie, a Scottish-born doctor who had decided in mid-life that he infinitely preferred designing golf courses to practising medicine. Jones had, in fact, recently played on one product of Mackenzie's genius – the lovely Cypress Point in California (see page 87).

The two men found that many of their ideas coincided. Jones wanted rapid, subtle greens, a course that his medium-handicap amateur friends could play but that would also test the tournament players. What a combination they made. A man with a proven flair for getting the best out of exciting terrain, and the greatest player the game had seen since Harry Vardon. The partnership could hardly fail. Jones called their creation Augusta National, and it proved to be everything he desired in a golf course.

In 1934, he decided to hold an informal tournament, based on invitation only, and called it the Augusta National Invitation. The title did not last the four days it took to play it. Newspapers were quick to christen it the Masters.

One thing that always surprises the first-time visitor to Augusta is just how hilly the course is. Television smoothes out the hillocks and gives the impression of a somewhat flat venue. Nothing could be further from the truth. The drive at the 18th, for example is steeply uphill. Conversely, the tee shot at the 10th plunges into a valley. Augusta favors the long hitters. With no rough and generous hitting areas, the powerful can open their shoulders safe in the knowledge that there is quite a margin for error. Or so it first appears. In fact, this is not really the case. For to be on the wrong side of the fairway at Augusta is to give yourself an often difficult shot to the green – and where your approach finishes on the greens largely dictates your score. This may seem a statement of the obvious. But whereas, on most courses, any professional with a modicum of putting ability would expect to get down in two

Seve Ballesteros wearing the Masters green jacket after his victory in 1980. The jacket ceremony is part of the Augusta tradition.

from anywhere on 'the dancefloor,' at Augusta this is by no means the case. To be above the hole at the 16th, for example, even by as little as 12ft, is likely to mean three putts far more often than one.

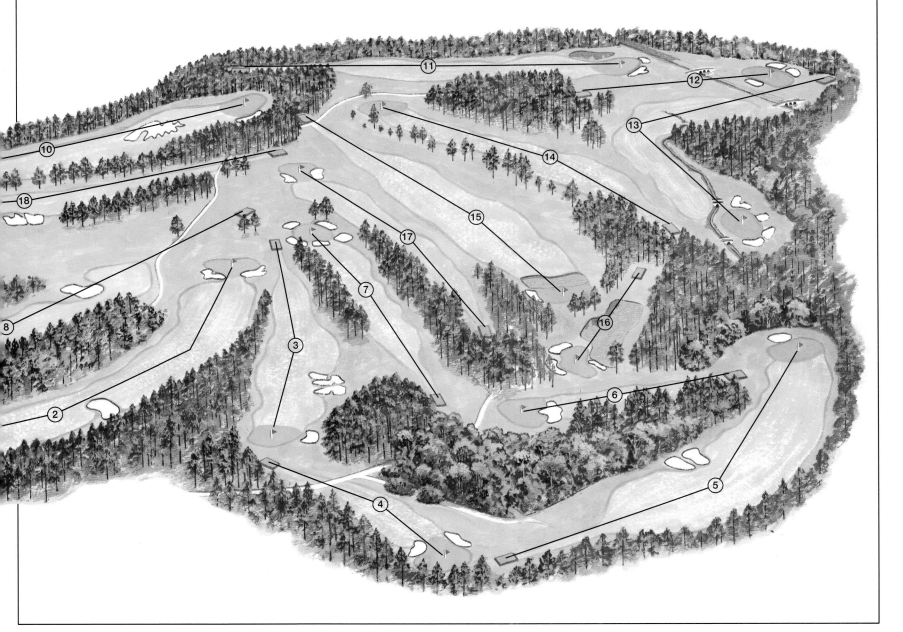

Amen Corner

Every year the Masters rushes to a crescendo of excitement over the last nine holes. And this is not simply because it is the conclusion of a major championship. The holes are designed specifically for this purpose. They are worth considering in detail, for each has a story to tell. The 10th is a par four, longer than the normal limit of 474 yards; but with the drive downhill, there is no problem in reaching the green in two. Ben Crenshaw did just that in 1984, and holed a 50ft birdie putt that

A vast and intimidating expanse of water lies in waiting before the 16th green. Many a contender's challenge has faltered at this hole.

set up his Masters triumph. By contrast, Scott Hoch missed from 18 inches in the first hole of a sudden death play-off to throw away his chance of the green jacket in 1989. The 11th begins the sequence known as Amen Corner, a name widely attributed to the writer Herbert Warren Wind, and so-called because players say 'Amen' if they negotiate it in par figures.

Larry Mize and Nick Faldo both won Masters titles in dramatic fashion at the 11th. In 1987 Mize chipped in to defeat Greg Norman at the second extra hole. Faldo was involved in dramatic play-offs in both 1989 and 1990. In the first he played a magnificent 3-iron into the heart of the green, then sank a 25ft birdie putt to win. And in 1990 his relentless golf again paid off at

the 11th when Ray Floyd dumped his approach shot into the water at the left front of the green.

The 12th, a par-three of little over 150 yards, is played to a wide but shallow green guarded by bunkers front and rear and by Rae's Creek at the front. Jack Nicklaus rates this as the most demanding short hole in championship golf. Sandy Lyle thought he had blown his chances in 1988 when, in the final round, after leading for 36 holes, he hit his tee shot into the creek and took five.

The 13th, a par-five, dog-legs left, a good tee shot leaving a long or medium iron approach to the green, which is also guarded by the creek.

One of the finest last-round efforts at Amen Corner was by the great Byron Nelson in 1937 when he gained no less than six shots on leader Ralph Guldahl by means of a birdie at the 12th and an eagle at the 13th on his way to a title-winning 66.

The Most Famous Shot

The 15th, another par-five, was the scene of the most famous shot in the history of the Masters. In 1935, Gene Sarazen came to the 15th tee trailing final-round leader Craig Wood by three shots. Sarazen hit a good drive which left him about 235 yards to the pin. He took out his favorite 4-wood, made perfect contact, and watched the ball soar over the pond fronting the green, make a soft landing – and roll unerringly into the hole for a double-eagle! Sarazen parred the last three holes and won the play-off the following day.

The 16th is another desperately difficult par-three. It's water all the way from tee to green. Lyle and Faldo both holed curling 12ft birdie putts here on their way to victory in 1988 and 1989 respectively.

The 18th is a seemingly straightforward par-four of 405 yards, but it has caused plenty of excitement down the years. In 1988, Sandy Lyle got the birdie he needed in spite of hitting his intendedly cautious 1-iron tee shot into the fairway bunker. Greg Norman, on the other hand, must detest the hole. In 1986, 1987 and 1989 he bogeyed the 18th when a par or better would have enabled him to win or tie the championship. But then, this magnificent course always seems to contrive a wonderfully exciting finish to the Masters.

An aerial view of Augusta National (right) which captures (l to r) the 7th, 6th, 14th, 15th, 16th and 5th holes.

BALLYBUNION

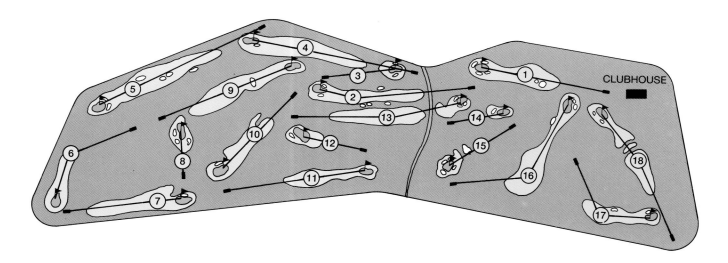

The remoteness of its location means that Ballybunion, north-west of Listowel in County Kerry, will never get the universal adulation and the television acclaim it deserves – for which, much thanks. There are some pleasures you just don't want to share with half the world. Ballybunion features in every self-respecting guide to the world's top 10 golf courses; some respected judges believe it to be without equal.

After visiting the course for the first time in 1971, Herbert Warren Wind wrote that Ballybunion 'revealed itself to be nothing less than the finest sea-

side course I have ever seen.' Tom Watson said: 'One can almost imagine that golf began here'; and any visit will surely confirm this impression.

Its architectural origins are something of a mystery, but whoever designed it did such a good job that when the club called in the English architect Tim Simpson in 1936 to remodel it, he made only cosmetic changes. Even these changes have not met with universal admiration. One, a double fairway bunker known as 'Mrs Simpson,' impedes the opening drive, although it was on the 14th fairway in Simpson's day.

Vision of Killashee

Towering sand dunes dominate the landscape skirting the Atlantic Ocean. The closeness of the sea means that while the course stands at a relatively modest 6,500 yards, there are days when it is totally unplayable. The place comes complete with a ruined castle plus the possibility of seeing the 'Vision of Killashee.' On rare calm days, in the sea near the Long Clare Peninsula people are seen to be walking along a bridge. The local guidebook observes: 'It lasts for about 15 minutes before it fades into nothingness, leaving the sea clear and blank as it was before.' Clearly the people in question are not golfers, otherwise they would be making straight for the 1st tee. Maybe they come from the old graveyard which lines the right-hand side of this hole and is an apt hazard on a course where many find their golf sinks without trace.

Together with the par-four 2nd and long par-three 3rd, it makes for a start as demanding as they come; but just as your spirits sag, along come two plain par-fives to revive your score.

Clifftop Golf

From the 423-yard 7th, the aesthetic qualities of the course soar as well. Your heart will miss a beat as you contemplate a second shot to a beautiful plateau green right above the roaring Atlantic. Alas, the march of time waits for no man or golf course. Erosion has

The second shot to the 385-yard 17th on Ballybunion's Old Course is a typical example of this pure links track.

The 216-yard par-three 15th. It is holes like this that led the eminent golf writer, Herb Warren Wind, to conclude that Ballybunion was the finest links course he had ever seen.

proved quite a problem here, and a replacement green has been built. This is an ongoing problem. In the 1970s a campaign was launched to save this precious piece of land and armed with the $200,000 collected, the 'friends of Ballybunion' helped to arrest the erosion at least for the present.

The 8th is a wonderful short hole, just 150 yards long, but as Watson said: 'One of the most demanding shots I have ever faced.' And so it continues along its heaven-made path. The 11th is another hole played directly along the clifftop: just clasp your hands together in prayer when playing this 450-yard brute on a windy day; the 14th and 15th are memorable short holes. The last three are all dog-leg holes, with the 18th possessing the perhaps unique distinction of a 'blind' shot for your last full stroke.

Perhaps that is not the fairest end to a golf course. Indeed, perhaps the course as a whole is not particularly fair. But, as one of its many admirers said: 'It may not be the truest form of golf but it is the form of golf I like most to play.'

A new clubhouse, and a further 18 holes were completed less than 20 years ago. The New course was designed by the American architect Robert Trent Jones, and it is so good it almost deserves comparison with the Old.

BALTUSROL

Situated an hour's drive from Manhattan, in Springfield, New Jersey, Baltusrol takes its name from a wealthy Dutch farmer, Baltus Roll, who owned the land 160 years ago. In 1831 he was murdered by thieves. Fortunately, the shots at Baltusrol today are of a more peaceful nature. And none more so than those played by the great Jack Nicklaus whose record at U.S. Opens played there reads: played two, won two. The first was in 1967 but the one that will always be recalled was in 1980, at a time when 'experts' thought they had detected a waning of his powers. Nicklaus had not won for two years, was approaching 40, and the argument ran that the most successful of golfing careers was drawing to a close. What the critics overlooked was that you don't use the criteria you apply to normal human beings on a man who had proven himself time and again to be anything but Joe Normal.

Jack's Wins

So it was that Nicklaus took his foot out of the grave with an opening round of 63. He set the pace from that point on and although there was the bravest of challenges from the Japanese Isao Aoki, Nicklaus was not to be denied. He received the most emotional of greetings on the 18th, and when he tapped in he had won by two strokes with a new championship record score of 272. 'I never want this day to end,' Nicklaus said in the press conference, as the enormity of his achievement (he had equaled the record of four Open wins) sunk in. By the end of it, the writers were almost pleading with him to leave so they could get on with the task of spreading the news to their readers.

Baltusrol's Lower course, the championship layout, was designed by A.W. Tillinghast, whose reputation for fair but challenging venues is strengthened by his work at Winged Foot in New York and Five Farms in Baltimore. Although a par 70 of more than 7,000 yards, it is not brute strength, as Nicklaus proved, that is required here. Tillinghast would have approved of such a winner as the Golden Bear for he wanted his course to reward the thinker and the shotmaker. Nevertheless, the course is not faultless. There has to be some question about a venue that has no par fives until the 17th, and then has two in succession.

Two Course Champion

The 1954 Open at Baltusrol produced an excellent quiz question; namely, who won the championship by playing two courses at the same time in his winning round? Answer, Ed Furgol. After driving into the woods on the 18th, Furgol's only method of escape was to play on to the Higher Course. He asked for a ruling and after an endless parade of officialdom, with second, third, and fourth opinions being called for, the Higher Course was finally declared to be not out of bounds. So Furgol played up the adjacent fairway, secured a birdie and won from Gene Littler by a shot.

Settling an Argument

For that 1954 Open, the architect Robert Trent Jones had been called in to toughen up Baltusrol. The most controversial aspect of his work centered on the 4th, which was already considered the best hole on the course. A par three, its fame had spread far and wide but Trent Jones was not impressed. He strengthened its defenses – and the club members were outraged. They considered it too tough. Trent Jones was not impressed by their protests either.

He offered to pay for any changes necessary out of his own pocket, and to settle matters, he, Johnny Farrell (the club professional at the time), the club chairman, and the chairman of the Open committee went out to play the hole. Jones watched while each played their shots. Then it was his turn. It was a beauty. His tee shot pitched just short of the flagstick, bounced once, and then gently rolled into the hole. Armed with probably the greatest argument-clincher the golf world has ever seen, Jones turned to his stunned companions and said: 'As you can see gentlemen, the hole is not too tough.'

The 18th green at Baltusrol is overlooked by a palatial clubhouse.

Jack Nicklaus pictured playing out of a bunker at the 4th during the second of his two US Open wins on this course.

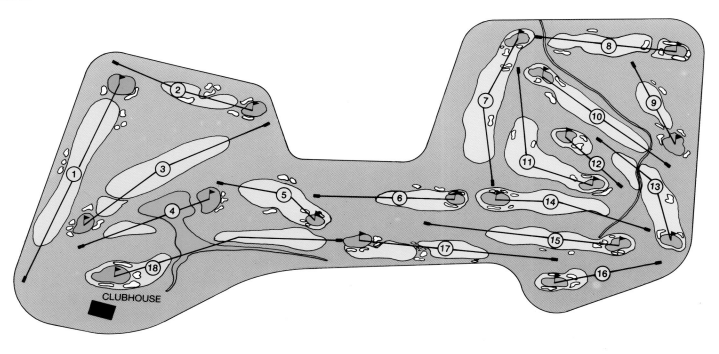

BANFF

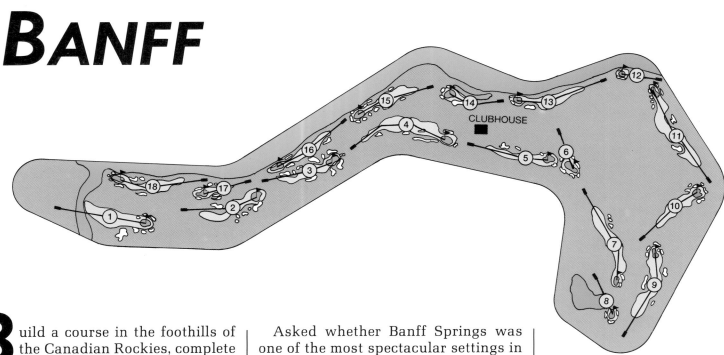

Build a course in the foothills of the Canadian Rockies, complete with two rivers and waterfalls, and surround it with a National Park game reserve so that deer and even a bear cub can be seen from time to time, and it is no wonder that people go on about Banff's enviable location.

Asked whether Banff Springs was one of the most spectacular settings in the world, the South African Bobby Locke replied: 'Not really. It is out of this world.' And indeed it is, a joyful romp with nature on a course that lives up to its spectacular setting.

Banff's first nine holes were built by the Canadian Pacific Railway Company to complement the awesome Banff Springs Hotel that looks down on the course; the second half was built by German prisoners during World War I. Not surprisingly the result was a somewhat crude realization of the possibilities that existed. In 1927, Stanley Thompson, the Canadian architect, gave Banff the golf course it deserved. He chopped down trees, he extracted tons of rock from the mountain, he imported topsoil from hundreds of miles away. All of which you would know only by reading about it: the finished article gives no hint whatsoever. It is simply breathtaking. The hole Thompson was proudest of, and indeed Banff's most famous hole, is the gorgeous par-three 8th, known as the Devil's Cauldron.

In a world which has its fair share of great par threes, this would certainly make any right-thinking person's top dozen. The 175-yard tee shot is over a natural miniature glacial lake to a green heavily protected by bunkers, and sloping towards the water. Behind the green, the trees rise to meet the imposing backdrop of Mount Rundle. Here, Thompson had to blast out the mountain wall to realise his vision. As someone once said, the hole demonstrates 'Thompson's uncanny knack for producing marvellous holes in rugged terrain.'

The enormous Banff Springs hotel was the original reason for the course being built and is a tourist attraction in its own right. They flock here, golfers and non-golfers alike.

CARNOUSTIE

The old saying about not knowing a good thing until it is gone certainly applies to Carnoustie. For years, the most satanic and starkly beautiful of British Open Championship venues was taken for granted — to the point where it started to show its age. Its condition left something to be desired, and after the 1975 event the state of the links, the lack of hotels in the area, the narrow access roads, and all other things that go to make the modern British Open roadshow, compelled the ruling body of the British game, Royal and Ancient, to take it off the Championship roster.

The sense of loss was felt immediately by the local residents who, aided by the wider business community sensing the commercial possibilities, have worked constructively to restore Carnoustie's reputation. At the end of the 80s, the R&A recognized the improvements and awarded Carnoustie the 1993 British Amateur Championship. It is highly likely that the final seal, the return of the Open, will follow within the decade.

A Course Without Weakness

If ever a course was a test of the best players of the day, then it is Carnoustie. It has been described as a course without a weakness, and with no consecutive holes following the same direction, the wind is an even greater factor than on other courses. Such are the fluctuations that you are quite likely to find the wind in your face on two successive holes, though with sunshine on one and a squally shower on the next. Given such circumstances it is hardly surprising that its British Opens have been won by the great players of the age.

In 1937 it was Henry Cotton who registered a rare British triumph. The British Open was not quite the event it is today, shorn as it frequently was of some of the best American players. But that year Cotton defeated the en-

tire U.S. Ryder Cup side, and on the final day defied torrential rain with a 71 — one of the great rounds of his career.

But if Carnoustie is ever associated with one player it is Ben Hogan who, in 1953, chose the course for his one British Open appearance, saw it, and conquered it. The great champion applied the principles of meticulous preparation that were a hallmark of his illustrious career. He practiced on it every day for a fortnight, studied it in every detail, and with the precision of a brain surgeon, carved out rounds of 73, 71, 70, and 68. Note the way that every round was better than the last. Hogan won by four shots. Hogan's record (he had already won the Masters and Open that year) had made him a living legend by the time he came to overwhelm the terrors of Carnoustie.

In 1968 the crowds flocked to Carnoustie for the British Open (above). Sadly they are no more but its reputation remains undimmed by the lack of recent exposure. An open and exposed course (right) — if the wind blows it is a place where golfers fear to tread.

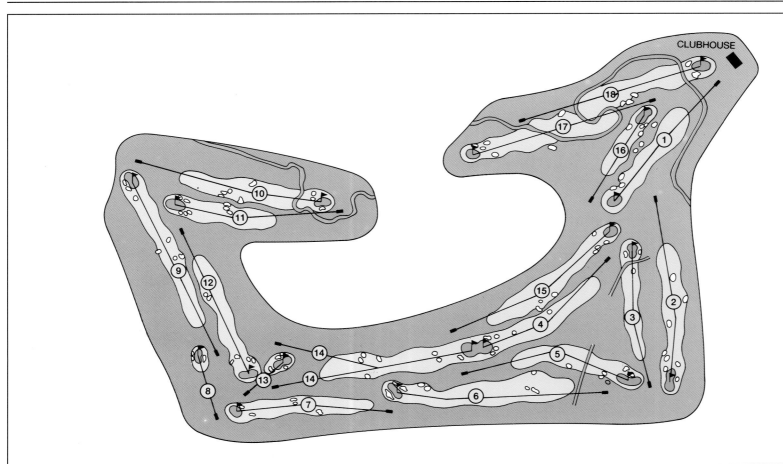

Large pot bunkers bordering the 15th are typical of what Carnoustie has to offer.

Watson's First Win

Strange as it seems now, another great player, Tom Watson, arrived for the 1975 Carnoustie British Open with something of a reputation as a player who faltered when the finishing line came into view. Carnoustie proved the making of him. Debut performances do not come any more impressive than his, as he triumphed after an 18-hole play-off against the Australian Jack Newton. Over the next eight years, Watson hardly gave any other player a chance when it came to Europe's most prestigious golf event.

Sandwiched between Watson and Hogan and completing a great triumvirate of post-war Carnoustie champions was Gary Player and his victory in 1968. Here, as ever, the challenge came from Jack Nicklaus, but the shot that won the event for Player came at the par-five 14th, a fairway wood over the 'spectacle' bunkers that finished three feet from the flag. The two shot advantage the eagle three gave Player proved the difference between the pair at the finish. From that hole onwards, Carnoustie's finish is recognized as being as tough as they come. Here we see the most pervasive influence of the Barry Burn, which sweeps through the course. On both the 17th and 18th holes it dissects the fairway twice, thus completing this most stringent of examinations.

It is to be hoped the British Open soon returns to Carnoustie. Anything else would be a betrayal, not only of a magnificent links, but of the 300 or more local residents who have turned professional over the generations and who spread the gospel of golf to the far flung corners of the world.

CHANTILLY

Nowhere is the game of golf expanding faster than in France. Once the pastime of wealthy aristocrats (especially English ones wintering in the south), it is now seeping through all sections of society and it will not be long before the country produces its own champion rather than reserve its adulation for Severiano Ballesteros. But in spite of all the new construction and all the new courses, la crème de la crème remains Chantilly. Situated some 25 miles north of Paris, its 36 holes have been carved out of magnificent woodland and nowhere is the modern world allowed to intrude. At Chantilly you can lose yourself as well as your ball.

The club was founded in 1908 under the presidency of Prince Murat and five years later the first of many French Opens were held on its championship course, which is known as the Vineuil. Such luminaries as Arnaud Massy, Henry Cotton, Roberto de Vicenzo (twice) and Nick Faldo have won the French Open at Chantilly over the years.

The Vineuil remains the most exacting of tests for even the best players. It stretches to 7,129 yards with a par of just 71 strokes. Nine of the par-fours are more than 400 yards, and three of the four par-threes are over 200 yards. Furthermore the two par-fives that close both the inward and outward halves measure no less than 576 and 596 yards respectively. Remember to bring your driver!

For all that, there has been some excellent scoring. In 1964, after a dry, hot summer, the course was playing short, and de Vicenzo and the South African Cobie LeGrange tied on 12 under par totals of 272. It was the graceful Argentinian who was to prevail, but only after five extra holes.

Chantilly's second 18 holes were designed by Tom Simpson, who was also responsible for the nearby and similarly classical Morfontaine. In the process, he redesigned the championship course, and while much of his work was damaged during the Second World War, enough survives to demonstrate how he enhanced the wonder of Chantilly.

At 596 yards, the par-5 home hole at Chantilly is one of the longest in championship golf. No choice but to take your driver here!

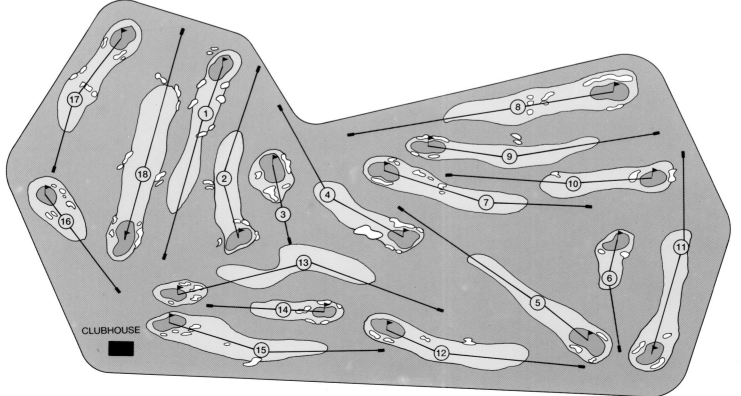

CLUBHOUSE

CLUB ZUR VAHR

The turn of the century ambition of August Weyhausen, the President of the multi-sport Club Zur Vahr, was to build a German championship course that would incorporate all the virtues of the great Scottish and English venues he had enjoyed so much. Few who play this delightful Bremen course would argue that he did not succeed.

After the 1971 German Open had been played there, the winner Neil Coles declared it among the very best in Europe. 'One could compare it to Augusta,' he said. 'The construction is very natural, and it is an excellent driving course, the par fives being particularly outstanding. Like all good courses, the finish is tough. The 230-yard 17th hole is the best par-three on the course, as you play through an avenue of trees, with out of bounds on the left. Altogether an excellent championship course – forcing you right to the limit.'

The Garlstedter Heide course was designed by Bernard von Limburger, and occupies 220 acres of thickly forested woodland. It is a big course, stretching beyond 7,200 yards with a par of 74. Limburger empathised with his surroundings to the extent that he cut down only the barest minimum of trees to lay fairways and greens. On most holes the tall pine trees run right to the fairway's edge.

There are only 24 bunkers simply because there is no need to lay any more. The course has ample natural hazards. The omnipresent pines can dominate the thinking of even the best. When he was competing in the 1971 German Open, the Argentine Roberto de Vicenzo was asked if it would help to have some fore-caddies to spot where the drives landed. 'No,' he said, 'the fore-caddies would get lost as well.'

The German Open returned to Club Zur Vahr in 1975 and 1985, although the last time was marked by severe thunderstorms and the tournament had to be reduced to 54 holes, with 1,100 yards chopped off the course's length. All's well that ends well, however. The winner was none other than the Kaiser of German golf himself, Bernhard Langer.

Dense pine forestation borders most of the holes at the Club Zur Vahr and calls for the straightest of drives to avoid disaster.

CYPRESS POINT

Dr Alister Mackenzie is talked about with all the reverence reserved for the game's legends. To describe Mackenzie as a golf architect is like describing Jack Nicklaus as a golfer. To have designed Augusta National alone would have secured for him a special place in the game's archives. That some years earlier he had carved out Cypress Point as well from the Monterey Peninsula is more than enough to inspire awe.

Cypress is not as challenging for the very top professionals as Augusta or indeed Pebble Beach, its near neighbor on the peninsula. But what it lacks in length or difficulty it more than makes up for in aesthetic appeal and charm. And, as on the classic links courses, there is always the unpredictable but

ever-present problem of the wind.

The 16th is undoubtedly the most photographed hole in the world and also one of the most talked about. Jutting out into the ocean, it is a par-three of 231 yards, nearly all of which is carry over the ocean if the green is to be reached. But this being Mackenzie, a prince among strategic as opposed to penal designers, there is more than one way to play the hole. Any golfer, be they a tournament pro or an 18-handicapper, can play his courses; the experience will be different in kind for each, but equally rewarding for both.

For those lacking confidence in their ability to hit a 200-yard shot across the bay from the 16th tee, there is the opportunity to play for the fairway, which lies less than half that distance away. It

may not lead to a par three, but neither will it pander to the Pacific's inexhaustible appetite for golf balls.

So difficult is this hole that in all the years it has been in existence, it has given up just 10 holes in one. One of these was scored by the late Bing Crosby, whose tournament, now known as the AT&T Pro-am, was played for every year at Cypress until 1991, and the adjoining Spyglass Hill and Pebble Beach. Another is Jerry Pate, whose pro-am partner on that particular day was Jack Lemmon. The actor recalls: 'Jerry was playing terribly, heading for a score in the low 80s, and he was still talking on his backswing, he was so mad with himself. He hit a 2-iron, and the damn thing went what looked like a mile out into the ocean. But he had hooked it and in it came, plunk, plunk, plunk, roll, straight into the cup. I have never heard any crowd reaction like it on a golf course. It was like a cannon went off.'

Naturally Gifted

But there is more to Cypress Point than one hole. Mackenzie was given 250 acres of the finest raw materials ranging from deep pine forests to huge soaring dunes and the purest of white sand. No finer compliment can be paid him than the fact that he did justice to such an environment — by tampering with it as little as possible. Among the other feature holes are the 3rd, another classic short hole, and the 5th, a gorgeous par-five, measuring 491 yards uphill through the pine forest. The 9th is another hole with a good deal of devil in it. Again there are two options. Downhill, the green is reachable in one but only if you are prepared to risk a greedy bunker on the left hand side and high grass at the back, should your ball run through the green. The safe option is a drive short, followed by a pitch and hopefully one putt.

Unlike Pebble, Cypress Point is not a public course. Indeed, it is one of the most exclusive clubs in America, with just 250 members drawn from all over the 50 states. It was the venue for the 1981 Walker Cup and it played a supporting role in the AT&T event. It seeks no championships and no publicity. But an invitation to play there is a privilege any golfer would be mad to forego.

The 15th hole at Cypress Point (right) measures just 143 yards but with the Atlantic on one side and bunkers everywhere, this is no simple iron shot. The even more famous 16th (below) requires a 200-yard shot across the bay if par is to be achieved.

DURBAN COUNTRY CLUB

I n golf, one man's misfortune is often another's gain. So it proved in the matter of golf courses in Durban in South Africa. In 1919 the premier club in Natal's capital was Royal Durban. But it was built on low-lying ground and there was embarrassment all round that year when the course became waterlogged during the national championship. The winner

Durban's fifth hole, like the first four, runs parallel to the ocean but it is the overhanging trees that cause all the problems. Everyone is content with a par here.

trawled his way round in 320 shots. The pressure to find a new venue was intense for otherwise it was feared Durban would fall off the golfing map. The result was Durban Country Club, designed by George Winterman and Laurie Waters, who won the South African Open four times between them.

The club first staged the national open two years after its completion in 1922, and the event has been held there many times since. Of all South Africa's 250 courses it is probably the one that is held in the highest esteem, and some of the nation's greatest players, including Bobby Locke and Gary Player, have enjoyed proud moments there. The

course saw Player's first South African Open success in 1956. When he returned there in 1969 he registered his seventh, his total of 273 including a record round of 64.

Although the course has been updated on several occasions, most recently by Bob Grimsdell in 1959, the layout has remained essentially unchanged. Everyone's favorite hole is the 3rd, which is played from an elevated tee at the highest point of the course into a valley. Equally dramatic is the 18th, which at 274 yards is one of the shortest of championship finishing holes, and which can be driven on a wind-free day. Woe betide, though, anyone who so much as fades the ball off center, for the right hand side gives on to a precipitous bank which will send the ball cascading down towards the practice ground. 'A little longer and the hole would be mediocre – just another drive and pitch,' said Grimsdell. 'But at this awkward and tempting distance, it is just the finish needed for a course which rewards good golf but ruthlessly exposes all our weaknesses.'

EMIRATES GOLF CLUB

The Emirates Golf Club in Dubai, the tiny city-state on the southern shore of the Persian Gulf, demonstrates the full range of man's ingenuity. To build a green oasis out of the harsh desert would be enough but to convert it into a fabulous test of golfing prowess is just breathtaking.

So are the logistics to keep this particular show on the road. Up to 750,000 gallons of water from the adjacent Gulf are desalinated daily and pumped via almost 19 miles of pipeline and 700 sprinklers on to the course, which has no fewer than five lakes. Without this watering, the course would revert to desert in two weeks.

The instigator of this most unlikely of all golfing projects was Sheikh Mohammed bin Rashid al Maktoum, the United Arab Emirates' Minister of Defense, whose affection for all sports is seen most vividly in his involvement in horse racing. His general plan involves turning Dubai into an international sports arena. Multi-million dollar cricket and field hockey stadia are to follow. The horse racing track, of course, was the first piece in this grand design.

The job of laying out the first grass golf course in the Gulf was handed over to the architect Karl Litten, who has designed courses all over the world but who believes this will come to be regarded as his masterpiece. To help the aesthetic process, thousands of trees were flown in. Royal palms from South America, date and coconut palms, Washingtonians, and giant Arizona cacti ring the fairways and greens. The clubhouse is a construction in keeping with the spectacular developments outside it – an extravagant cluster of concrete buildings shaped like gigantic bedouin tents. It cost $10 million alone to build, and there has never been a clubhouse that so brilliantly reflects its surroundings.

Within 18 months of opening, the Emirates Club was declared not only good enough for the European Tour but also lauded by all those professionals who made the lengthy journey. The inaugural Desert Classic was won by the Englishman Mark James, who promptly pronounced it as good a course as the professionals would play on all year – a view endorsed by Irishman Eamonn Darcy, who set a new course record during his 1990 victory.

No, it is no mirage but a sensational aerial view of the miraculous Emirates course in Dubai. Without water, they reckon all this would be returned to the desert within a month.

GLENEAGLES

For the club golfer, as distinct from the tournament player, a primary factor when choosing his favorite courses must be location. The best layout in the world he is going to find pretty mundane if it is stuck in the middle of an industrial park. But place a course (even if it does have one or two eccentricities), not to mention limitations, in the middle of one of the most beautiful Scottish glens, and all is forgiven. Such is the fare on offer at the King's Course at Gleneagles. It was designed by James Braid, but really it is the fair hand of nature which makes it all worthwhile. Where the holes are not lined by vast plumes of gorse and heather there are tall firs and pine, beech and elder. In season you will hear the call of the wild geese, grouse and pheasant. In or out of season you will hear the cries of the odd golfer or two in extremis.

The course, together with its world-famous hotel, was opened just after World War I, with Braid coming up with a design which matched his brief. 'Make it spectacular. Make it look difficult, but make it easy to get around,' he was told. With a course record standing at 62, José-Maria Olazábal certainly fulfilled the last criterion.

British television's coverage of celebrity pro-ams or the Scottish Open has made the course well known all over Britain. The most famous, and probably the best hole is the 13th. This par-four of 448 yards is known as Braid's Brawest (bravest) and it was his favorite. A ridge with an intimidating bunker in its face cuts the fairway at 200 yards and must be carried if the green is to be reached in two. The second shot is to a plateau green which slopes from left to right.

The bunkered ridge on the 13th is merely a spur of a much longer ridge that is involved in almost every hole. On some holes the tee is on one side of the ridge and the green on the other. On many such holes – the 374-yard 3rd, for instance – the approach shot will be blind; a feature of older golf course design that is frowned on today. At Gleneagles, however, it hardly affects the player's enjoyment. For even if he is off his game, there is always the breathtaking scenery to enjoy.

Take the high road or the low road it makes no difference. All roads round Gleneagles lead to fabulous scenery and in the middle of it all is a golf course to do it justice.

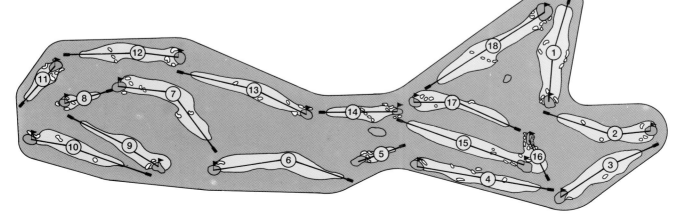

KASUMIGASEKI

When two Japanese golfers won the World Cup for the host nation at Tokyo's greatest course, Kasumigaseki, in 1957 they ensured immortality for themselves and the venue. Torakichi Nakamura and Koichi Ono are widely credited for the explosion of interest in the sport in Japan, to the extent that as many as one in ten now play golf. Play in this sense, however, is a relative term. Most have to make do with hitting golf balls all their lives on three-tier driving ranges, since rigid planning restrictions mean there is not enough land to build sufficient courses, while the average price of a club membership stands at over $100,000. Even then there is a waiting list of several years.

Kasumigaseki's standing as the most famous course in the country may have been earned on the back of that World Cup triumph but it is richly deserved. The more famous East Course was designed by a talented Japanese amateur Kinya Fujita, and although the design itself was fine, his lack of knowledge of golf architecture was apparent in places. The English designer Charles Alison was brought in to dramatize his layout, and he studded the course with deep, cavernous bunkers that are two-a-penny in Scotland but were a revelation to the Japanese. To this day, such deep bunkers are known as 'Alisons'.

The Japanese talent for landscaping and decoration is evident everywhere with over 200 people employed to keep the two courses in immaculate condition. For the greenkeepers, there is the additional and uniquely Japanese burden of having two greens on each hole to tend. One is sown with rye and bent grasses, which cannot withstand the withering Japanese summers, so another is carpeted with Korai grass, from Korea, which can. People keep telling the Japanese that hybrid grasses are now available and one green is all that is really necessary, but they have got used to such methods and few clubs dare offer anything else.

Straight and Narrow

The Japanese reputation for short game excellence is founded on the principle that if you can master Korai grass, where the grain grows in all directions, you can overcome anything. In the 1957 Canada Cup, Nakamura was supreme in this area, holing everything and never once failing to get down in two from an 'Alison.'

The Englishman Alison is one of the most respected of all architects and Kasumigaseki is characteristic of his work. His simple philosophy was that the player who follows the straight and narrow should be rewarded with a relatively untroubled path to the green, and so he saved his sandtraps for the wild hitters.

Perhaps the finest hole on the course is the last which measures 483 yards and is one of those that should really

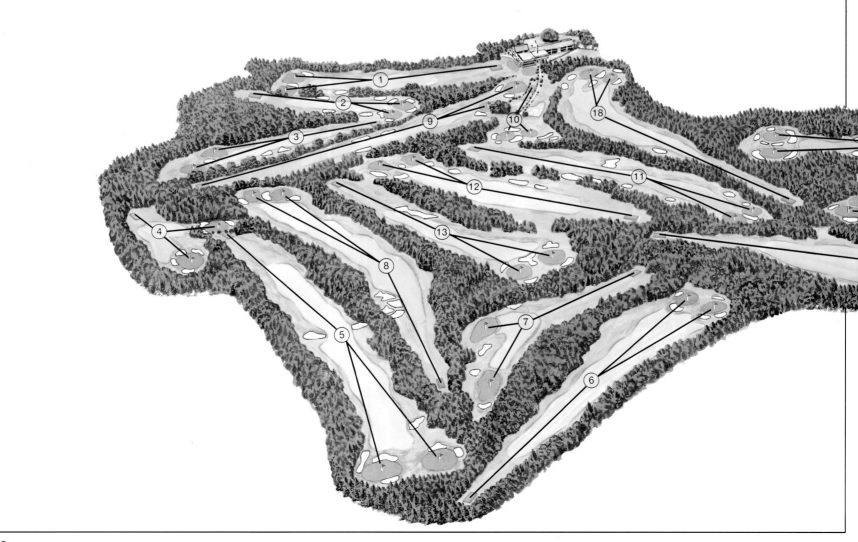

Right: The 9th hole with the clubhouse in the background. Note the impeccably trimmed hedges and trees, and the deep 'Alison' bunkers.

Below: Eric Brown of Scotland driving at the 1st during the 1957 Canada Cup. Japan won the cup and the Japanese golf boom was launched.

have a par of $4\frac{1}{2}$ for the top players. A dog-leg right, the drive offers an irresistible temptation for the big-hitter since the green is perfectly reachable in two shots. As with all great par-fives, a second shot of singular quality is needed if the green is to be located. From the ideal drive, the line is across the deepest expanse of a valley while the entrance to the green is guarded by intimidating bunkers.

The second course at Kasumigaseki is an enviable asset too, for the fortunate few who are members. Again Fujita was involved, this time in collaboration with Seichi Inoue. Completed in 1931, it followed the example set by Alison to assure the venue's spot in any guide to the World's great courses.

KILLARNEY

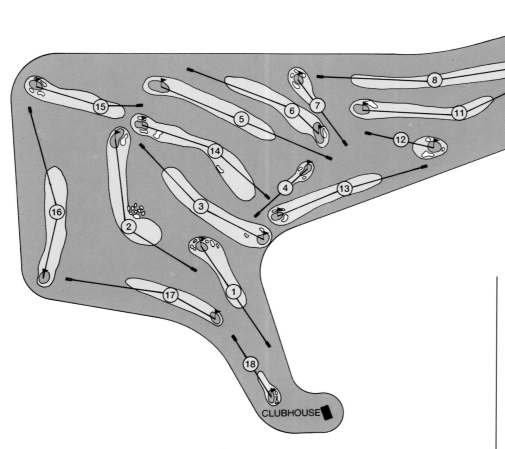

Any golfing pilgrimage to Ireland must include a visit to Killarney. Situated on the banks of Lough Leane, with MacGillicuddy's Reeks creating a thrillingly imposing backdrop, Killarney – as the distinguished British golf journalist Pat Ward-Thomas once wrote, 'exhausts superlatives.' Killarney Golf and Fishing Club was born as recently as 1971, exciting no little controversy. Then a second course was added, with the new 36-hole layout made up of an intermingling of the two.

The traditionalists were less than pleased at this tampering with what they regarded as perfection. The original 18 had been laid by the noted architect Sir Guy Campbell, in collaboration with the owner, Viscount Castlerosse, who invited his close friend Henry Longhurst to contribute suggestions. Castlerosse continued to refine and develop after Campbell had finished and it was his ambition eventually to install such extravagantly colored shrubs as he had seen at Augusta, Georgia. His untimely death in 1943 put an end to that.

The club reclaimed some land while the Irish Tourist Board bought sufficient ground for a further nine holes. Fred Hawtree was called in, and his utilization of land near the lake means that water comes into play much more, not to mention spectacular new views of the lake and mountains.

Killarney has attracted only a small number of tournaments and championships and when it does, a composite course of the two layouts, Killeen and Mahony's Point, is used. One of the most notable holes is the 18th, an unconventional finish since it is a par-three. At 202 yards it demands length, and accuracy: the shot must carry the shore of the lake, while there is little margin for error on the left, where there is a long, thin bunker and a road. The green, indeed, is a delightful emerald oasis framed by bushes and pine trees and, beyond, the lake and the dark line of the mountains. As Longhurst, who knew it in all its moods, observed: 'What a lovely place to die!'

A typical Killarney scene as the dying embers of the day's sun reflects across the lakeland waters and casts long shadows across the fairways.

MERION

Hugh Wilson's career as a golf architect was tragically terminated after just one work, when he died at the age of 46. Such is the stature of that one masterpiece, however, that the migrant Scot will never be forgotten. For he was the creator of Merion, in the fashionable Philadelphia suburb of Ardmore, one of America's finest courses.

Wilson was a graduate of Princeton, a local insurance broker, and member of a committee of Merion members delegated to oversee the development of an abandoned farm and old stone quarry that had been bought to build a golf course, their old one having become obsolete. It quickly became clear that Wilson was the creative and artistic director of the project, and he was sent

back to his native Scotland, where he spent several months making drawings and maps. Wilson incorporated all that he saw and heard into a course of distinction and beauty that was completed in 1912. There were 128 bunkers, quickly named 'the white faces of

Merion' since they had been filled with the glaring sand of the abandoned quarry.

The site is but 110 acres (most architects consider 200 acres the minimum requirement these days) and at a shade over 6,500 yards it is far shorter than all the other courses used by the United States Golf Association for the Open. And yet the USGA keep returning to it because Merion has invariably produced winners capable of meeting the demands it makes on premium shotmaking and consummate putting ability. There cannot be anything

Right: This plaque at Merion confirms Bobby Jones's immortality as the only player ever to do the Grand Slam. Below: The clubhouse at Merion, which has overseen many of golf's most memorable deeds. No doubt there will be more to come with an imminent return for the US Open.

wrong with a course that boasts Bobby Jones, Ben Hogan, Jack Nicklaus and Lee Trevino among its champions. At least two of those occasions witnessed truly memorable moments in American golf. Jones won two of his record five Amateur titles at Merion. It is the second of these which always remembered. It formed the fourth, and last, event of what he called the 'impregnable quadrilateral' – the British and United States Opens and Amateur Championships, which he won in 1930.

Hogan's Miracle

Twenty years later Hogan won the most emotional Open of them all. A year earlier he had been involved in an horrific car accident that had left him fighting for his life. His injuries from the head-on collision included a broken collarbone, ankle, pelvis, and rib, not to mention internal injuries. Yet here he was, less than 12 months on, play-

ing in the Open, and after two rounds he was in contention. The problem for Hogan was that his injuries had not completely healed. Every night he went back to his hotel room and would lie in the bath for an hour to try and soothe the pain from his aching legs. Hogan possessed the most relentlessly competitive edge the game has known, but he doubted if would be able to get through 36 holes the next day.

He got his caddy to pick his ball out of the hole, while his playing partner, Cary Middlecoff, sportingly marked it on the greens. Gradually, a miracle evolved. With six holes to play, Hogan had carved out a three-hole lead. Having tip-toed to the brink of glory, however, he thought he could do no more. He almost collapsed at this point. He started to drop shots, and when he came to Merion's most formidable finishing hole, he needed a par-four to tie Lloyd Mangrum and George Fazio. Hogan conjured up the deepest re-

serves of his courage to strike an imperious 1-iron to the heart of the last green to make the play-off. His face was etched with the distress of a long distance runner who collapses on reaching the tape. But the next day he had a second wind, he won the play-off and the second of his four Opens.

In 1971, Merion was the scene of Trevino's emphatic arrival on to the world class stage. He defeated Nicklaus in a play-off to claim the title.

One of the men Hogan had defeated for his win, Fazio, is now one of the top American architects, so he is well qualified to assess the merits of Merion. He rates it alongside Pine Valley as the kind of course he most admires. 'It has character,' he said. 'It is challenging without being back breaking.'

The 11th hole. It was here, by an 8&7 margin in the final, that Bobby Jones won the US Amateur in 1930.

MID OCEAN

No course was ever more evocatively named than Mid Ocean, the jewel of that beguiling island in the western reaches of the Atlantic, Bermuda. With New York standing just 90 minutes' flight time away, generations of Americans have come to appreciate its captivating beauty and stern challenge to their golfing prowess.

The course was designed by that great pioneer of American golf, Charles Blair Macdonald, who studied at St. Andrews, Scotland, and then returned home determined to put everything into practice that he had learned. Many consider The National at Southampton, Long Island, to be his masterpiece, but Mid Ocean, if only for the glory of its setting, would probably get the vote of many more non-purists. It begins with two great par-fours in the first five holes. The 1st hole runs almost to the ocean shore and is appropriately called Atlantic. But it is the 5th which has helped spread the name of Mid Ocean far and wide.

This is one of those holes where the architect has made a pact with the devil. All along the left hand side runs Mangrove Lake, and the player has to use his sense of feel to determine how much of the water he can carry with his tee shot. The greater his sense of daring – and always assuming he does not finish in the lake – the easier becomes his second shot to the large but well-bunkered green. With the hole running to 433 yards, a sense of adventure needs to be exercised if the approach is not to run to something like a 2- or 3-iron. Timidity, and a bail out drive to the right, turns the hole into an almost certain bogey.

Nevertheless, despite these two stringent examinations, the first eight holes represent the easy bit and any score has to be made over this stretch. From the 9th through to the 15th might be termed the heart of the course. The first of these holes presents an intimidatingly long carry over water from the tee, while the 13th is a par-three measuring 238 yards.

Macdonald was an exponent of the penal, as opposed to strategic, philosophy of golf course architecture. In its purest form, this involves allowing the golfer only one viable route from tee to green, and punishing him severely if he deviates from it, even if only slightly. Mid Ocean represents a somewhat mellow version of this philosophy, though the 5th hole is a reminder of how testing the game can be – even in this idyllic setting.

The 5th hole at Mid Ocean. A spectacular dog-leg. It asks a classic golf question – how much do you dare to gamble?

MUIRFIELD

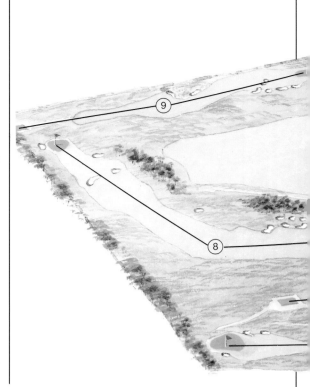

Muirfield is the jewel in a string of fine courses that line the southern shore of the Firth of Forth between Edinburgh and Dunbar in Scotland. 'The course is built in the right proportions,' said Nick Faldo of the course where he won the 1987 British Open. 'When you have a long shot to the green, the green is generous enough. When you face a small shot, the target is small too.'

Muirfield is recognized as one of the fairest of links courses but the punishment can be savage for the errant shot. This is an example of the punishingly deep sand traps.

It was not always this way. Indeed, in the early days Muirfield came in for a lot of criticism. In *Historic Golf Courses of the British Isles*, published in 1910, the noted British writer Bernard Darwin commented: 'Muirfield has had a checkered career in regard to public opinion and at times has been very violently abused.' He added: 'The Open was for the first time played for at Muirfield in 1892 and it is possible that the course was hardly good or long enough for a championship course.' When the world's finest golfers return in 1992 for the centenary of that first Muirfield Open, they will

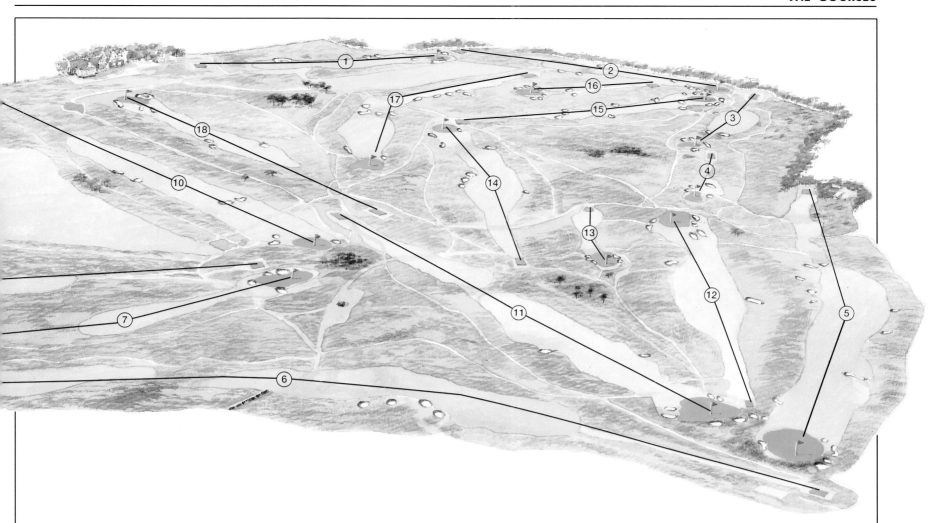

find that if the course was too easy once, it certainly is not any more.

That first Muirfield British Open was memorable for several reasons. It was played for the first time over 72 holes instead of 36 and it was won by an amateur, Harold Hilton, of Hoylake, England. That is something we can safely say will not happen in 1992!

The course we know today essentially came into being in 1925 when the great Wentworth architects Harry Colt and Tom Simpson were brought in to make changes. One of Muirfield's outstanding features is the bunkers, described by Nicklaus as: 'The most fastidiously-built bunkers I have ever seen, the high front walls faced with bricks of turf fitted together so precisely you would have thought a master mason had been called in.' Some professionals are rather less poetic when they discover their ball has landed in one. At best it means a shot dropped, at worst...well, anything can happen. Who can forget the sight of Arnold Palmer huffing and puffing while trying to get out of one during the 1987 British Open?

Open Drama

The most famous holes on the course are the 10th, one of the great par-four holes in British golf, and the closing two holes, which have seen all sorts of drama down the years. In 1972, the 17th was the scene of perhaps the most dramatic

of all conclusions to an Open. It starred the defending champion Lee Trevino and the British hero of the hour, Tony Jacklin. Going into the hole, Supermex held a one stroke lead, but it appeared

Muirfield may look toothless from the air but this is the safest way by far to view its man-eating sandtraps.

The long range spectators peer into the distance as Nick Faldo achieves instant fame by winning his first British Open at Muirfield.

that Jacklin would prevail. Trevino, for just about the first time in his life, had started hooking. He hooked his drive, he chipped out, he hooked his third shot. His fourth shot finished through the green. He was looking at a six at best. Jacklin, meanwhile, was heading for a four. He had hit the perfect drive, an equally immaculate second shot, and now was just 30 yards short of the hole. Even when he played an extremely poor pitch shot, the ball coming up 18ft short of the hole, there was no hint of the drama that was still to unfold. Trevino walked nonchalantly to his ball. Coming down the fairway he had told Jacklin that he hoped Jacklin would go on to win because he himself was down and out.

We can take it that that was a piece of 'kidology' on Trevino's part to try and gee himself up. At any rate, his chip from the rough was perfect, running gently into the hole. Now Jacklin had to hole his putt to tie Trevino going

to the final hole. He missed, then he missed the return as well.

In 1987, a home player was once more in contention and he too was trailing by one shot playing the next to last hole. But this time it was Paul Azinger who ran up a bogey, and when he failed to secure par at the last as well, Nick Faldo had realized his dream. He did so in splendid fashion. The 18th is probably the most demanding finishing hole in British Open Championship golf. But Faldo played it faultlessly, illustrating the improvements in his swing that had taken two years out of his professional life. He secured a par – the 18th, moreover, of his round. Par excellence, indeed.

That British Open was an example of how tough Muirfield can play. There was practically no wind that day, but almost alone among the great links courses, Muirfield does not need any to defend itself. The day was cold, the rain had fallen all week, and the haar (sea-mist) had rolled in off the Forth estuary. All of which was more than enough insurance.

If there is a criticism of Muirfield it is that in some respects it is soulless.

There are horror stories, like the one of Tom Watson being chased off the course the day after a British Open, because by then the private club was back in the hands of the members. This august body is the Honourable Company of Edinburgh Golfers, which came into being in 1744, thereby predating the Royal and Ancient by 10 years. Some of them still think it is 1744. There never has been a Muirfield professional, for example.

For all that, it cannot be denied that they have a magnificent golf course which is always in supreme condition. Herbert Warren Wind probably put it best: 'Muirfield's great quality is its frankness – its honesty. There are no hidden bunkers, no recondite burns, no misleading and capricious terrain. Every hazard is clearly visible. Chiefly for this reason, the course has always been extremely popular with foreign golfers and especially Americans; it has a sort of "inland" flavour that makes visitors feel much more at home on it than on any other British championship course. Moreover, Muirfield is perhaps the most beautifully conditioned course in Britain.'

MUIRFIELD VILLAGE

Sandy Lyle plays out of one of the fearsome sandtraps and hopes to carry another on his way to the 5th green.

Over the past 20 years or so Jack Nicklaus, not content with being the best golfer in the world, has become one of the most distinguished golf architects of his day. But while Nicklaus courses can now be seen in most places where golf is played, it is doubtful if he will improve on one of the first he designed with the help of architects Pete Dye and Desmond Muirhead. In a recent *Golf Digest* feature on the 100 best United States golf courses, Muirfield Village was judged to come seventh overall.

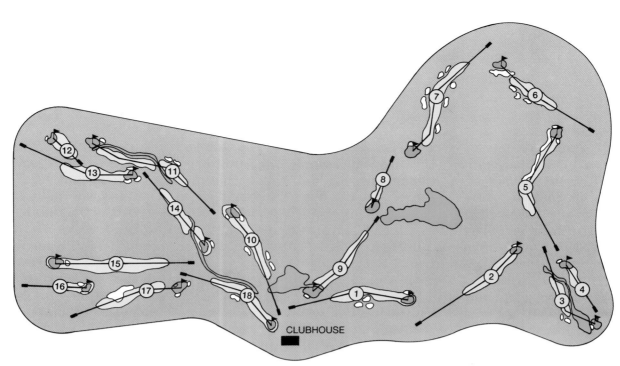

The 16th hole at Muirfield Village reflects Jack Nicklaus's admiration of the work done by Alister Mackenzie at Augusta National.

All of which was some achievement for a course that at the time was less than 15 years old.

Nicklaus named the course after the great Scottish links where he won his first British Open Championship in 1966. The two courses have absolutely nothing in common, except his excellence. No, in terms of design, Nicklaus's inspiration was another of his favorite pieces of real estate: he wanted to create a northern interpretation of Augusta National near his home town of Columbus, Ohio. Indeed, if you stand on the par-three 12th at Muirfield Village, you could (almost)

be standing on the par-three 16th at Augusta, so faithfully does it copy its characteristics.

When Jack told his then manager, Mark McCormack, of his plans to build the course, the latter dissolved into fits of laughter, and told him he would bankrupt himself. But Jack did not win 20 major titles by giving up that easily. He went ahead even though the price of the land jumped up from $900 to almost $5,000 an acre when it was learned that the hand of Nicklaus was involved. It was thought it would cost $1.6 million. The eventual total was considerably nearer $4 million than $2 million.

Since then more than 100 amendments have been made to the original design. Nicklaus has never been afraid to admit mistakes and learn from them. Of course, it helps if you have an ex-

ceedingly deep pocket. At the 11th, for example, the original design called for a stream cutting across the fairway at about 320 yards from the tee. The stream then continued along the right side of the fairway, before turning left and feeding into a lake, which protected the entire front of the green. When Nicklaus played the hole he realized that from the landing area of the drive, the lake could not be seen. So he had the lake filled in and now all that is left is the narrow stream. That one operation is said to have cost $200,000.

All the expense must feel worth it each spring, when Nicklaus plays host to one of the great events on the tour, the Memorial Tournament. And in particular, his chest must have swelled with pride at all the praise engendered by the hosting of the 1987 Ryder Cup.

Unfortunately for Jack, Muirfield Village will also be remembered as the place where Europe finally won the Ryder Cup on United States soil. Just to make it worse for the great man, he was not only the host, but also the captain of the losing side. Nicklaus took it all with the good grace that has been a hallmark of his career. He did not overcriticize his own players, preferring instead to recognize a courageous European team that contained some exceptional players whose time had come. And the venue itself proved the most worthy of stages. The first morning of the contest was memorable, the dew still glistening on the lawn-like fairways, the trees dancing as the sunrise brought out their Autumn hues of every shade of brown, red, and gold. Nowhere in golf does a creative collaboration of man and nature revel more delightfully in its splendor than at Muirfield Village.

PEBBLE BEACH

There are many who assert that Pebble Beach on the Monterey Peninsula in California is the finest championship course in the world. If your bottom jaw does not drop open the first time you encounter the ocean holes at Pebble, then you are barely alive.

Yet Pebble Beach has held only two Opens, with one to follow in 1992. Principally this was because of accommodation problems: the region was once the exclusive enclave of millionaires. Thankfully, recent resort development has gone ahead without too much damage to the area's extreme beauty. And

we can take it as read that quite a few more Opens will follow in the years ahead.

The course was first brought to national prominence by Bing Crosby, who had started his own pro-am event in 1936, and moved it from Los Angeles to Monterey in 1947. It is still held today, although sadly the Crosby name has now been discarded in favor of that of the latest corporate sponsor, AT&T.

An aerial view of one of the finest pieces of golfing real estate in the world.

Golden Bear's Honeypot

The two Opens at Pebble have been special indeed. They both featured the greatest player of the past 30 years, Jack Nicklaus. Indeed the Golden Bear has figured in practically every national event that has been staged at the venue. His love affair with Pebble began in 1961 when he dominated the Amateur. He was no less than 20 under par for the 112 holes he played that week, and was never over par in any of his seven matches. Nicklaus won the inaugural Open played there in 1972 and was runner-up a decade later at the second. In 1977 he finished third in the one PGA Championship played on the course to date.

The ocean holes begin after three fairly routine holes to start. The 4th is a fine short par-four, the 5th an excellent par-three that turns inland and runs uphill into a wooded area. Course designer Jack Neville wanted it to run along the clifftop, but the owner had sold a plot of land there and the buyer declined to sell it back to him.

There follows a five-hole stretch of clifftop golf with Pebble Beach in all its splendor. The second shot at the 6th, above Stillwater Cove, has for its target a plateau green on the peninsula spearing out into Carmel Bay. The 7th, at 110 yards, is the shortest hole in American championship golf (and, with Cypress Point's 16th, the most photographed), but this being Pebble, there is nothing small about its stature. It may be simply a flick with a wedge, but it is to a green below that is dramatically guarded, with rocks and ocean spray also a factor, not to mention the wind swirling in off the Pacific.

A Great Par-Four

The 8th, one of the great par-fours in championship golf, calls for a drive up-hill to a plateau just over the horizon from the tee. Then the golfer is faced with one of those death-or-glory choices. He has now only about 180 yards to go — but between him and the green the ocean has taken a gigantic bite out of the fairway, leaving an aching, windswept chasm that plunges to the rocks on the shore. The question is: does he go for the green risking an all-too-likely perdition; or, if not, how much of the chasm will he dare to carry by hitting left onto the fairway but far short of the green? And, if he does play safe, he must bear in mind that his third shot, a pitch to the green, is downhill and very often, downwind as well, and that the green is small and bunkered at sides and back. In wind, anyone who pars this hole knows his game.

The 9th and 10th, both longish par-fours, are a connoisseur's delight in their classical simplicity and the mixture of power and finesse they require of even the finest players. The 9th runs downhill to the green, but in addition the fairway slopes from left to right —

The par-5 18th hole. 548 yards and bending left around the curve of the beach, it is one the best finishing holes in championship golf.

towards the cliffs. Most golfers, especially those with a natural fade, line their drive to the left, which lengthens the hole's already more-than-adequate 450 yards. The slightly shorter 10th is much the same shape, but its fairway at the range of the average drive from the tee is narrowed by bunkers on the left to little more than 30 yards; and, like the 9th, its green is perched on the edge of the ocean.

The course now turns inland, weaving its way through woodlands of cypress, oak, eucalyptus, and Monterey pine before heading back towards the ocean. Its two finishing holes are among the finest and most testing of any championship course. The 17th is a par-three, but at 218 yards and usually played into the wind, it requires a long iron (at least) of pinpoint accuracy. In the 1964 Crosby Pro-Am, Arnold Palmer misjudged the wind to such a degree that he cleared the green and the rough behind it and ended up on the beach; he took nine. In the 1972

Open, Jack Nicklaus hit a magisterial 1-iron that covered the flag all the way, hit the pin and stopped six inches from the hole. And Tom Watson effectively won the same event 10 years later by chipping into the hole from the greenside rough (see page 66).

The 18th is a superlative scimitar-shaped par-five of 540 yards. To the left the beach threatens any attempt to take to great a short cut with drive or second shot, and at the end the curv-

The 7th hole at Pebble Beach is straight out of fantasy island with the waves of the Pacific Ocean crashing away in the background.

ing fairway slopes uphill to the green. In his 1982 triumph Watson tamed this monster with a 3-wood, a 7-iron, a 9-iron, and a 20-foot putt that in truth he had intended to lay up but which toppled into the hole for a magnificent birdie.

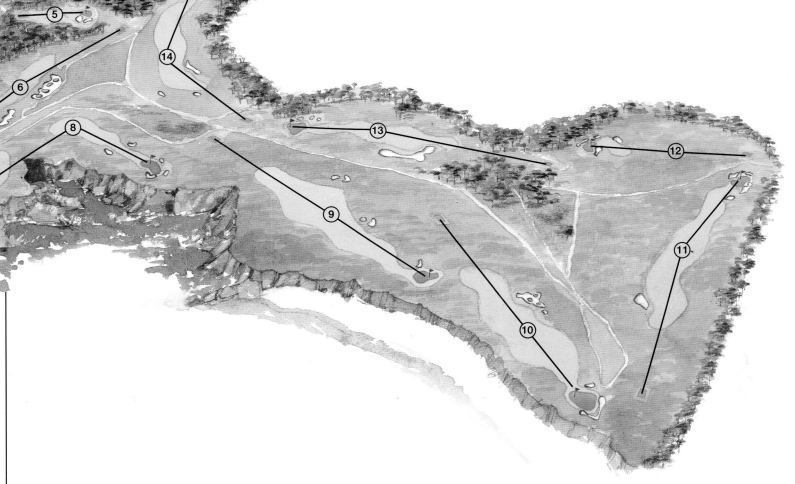

PINEHURST No 2

With a different golf course for every day of the week, it is no surprise that Pinehurst is regarded in some quarters as Utopia. A small community of no more than 3,000 people, it is situated on the North Carolina sandhills, a freak of geography dating back to the ice age. The No 2 course, designed by Donald Ross, is anything but a freak of nature. This is the jewel in the Pinehurst crown, a course whose appeal was summed up by Tommy Armour thus: 'The man who does not feel emotionally stirred when he plays golf at Pinehurst should be ruled out of golf for life.'

Pinehurst was the creation of Bostonian James Tufts at the turn of the century. He wanted to start a winter resort for New Englanders of modest means. The village betrays its founder's taste and roots for it could quite easily be fitted into Connecticut, Maine or Ver-

mont. Tufts bought 5,000 acres and so when he became intrigued by this new game that everyone was referring to as golf, he had the ideal territory with which to satisfy his curiosity. Pinehurst No 1 was a crude prototype, but two events in 1900 shaped the region's future. In March, Harry Vardon – who, a few months later won the U.S. Open – stopped by to play four rounds, thereby whetting the appetite of the local community. And in December, Tufts appointed Donald Ross, a Scot from Dornoch, as resident professional.

A Masterpiece

Within his first year, Ross began work on the first nine holes of what is now known throughout the world as the No 2 course. He completed the 18 holes in 1907 and so great was his achievement it was immediately recognized as a masterpiece, even though it stretched

to only 5,800 yards. Over the years, Ross constantly refined and modernized his work and today it measures over 7,000 yards.

Unlike many of the better American inland courses, Pinehurst has just one water hazard, at the 16th, where a small pond has to be carried some 180 yards from the tee. The beauty of the course is that since Tufts carved out the original site, the natural woodland has reclaimed most of its territory, leaving every hole in its own natural setting. Each hole therefore has its own charm, its own distinct character, and no two are alike.

Ross's Scottish and, specifically, Dornoch ancestry is evident in certain places with mounds a distinctive feature of the approaches to the greens. This is obvious on holes like the 8th, a gorgeous par-four of 464 yards where the tee shot plunges into a long valley whence the fairway rises to a slightly

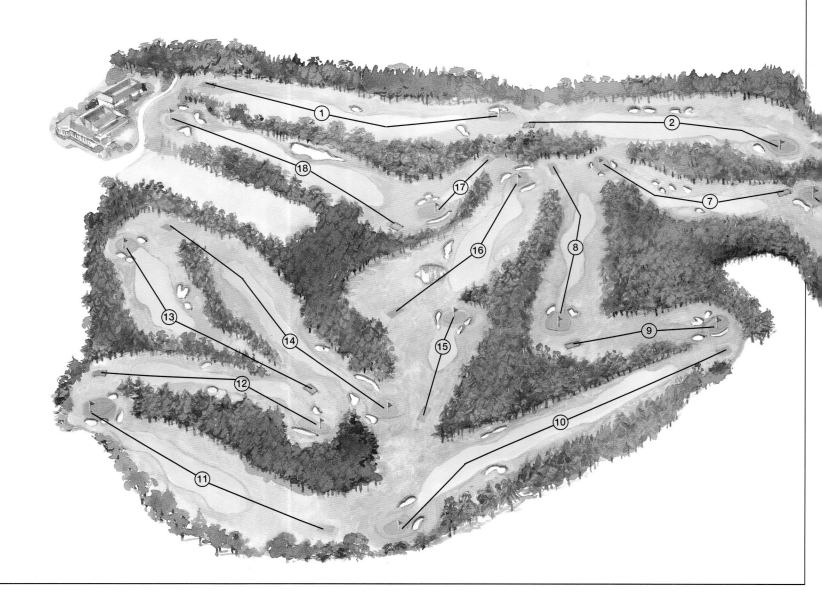

elevated green. Another Scottish trait was to leave the greens bereft of a collar of rough which is such a feature of American courses. Ross believed that such a penalty was too harsh for a shot that might have missed the green by no more than inches. Instead he preferred to demand recovery strokes that would be considerably less difficult but would make the player think. Because of its remote location, and the difficulty of accommodating crowds along the fairways and around the greens, Pinehurst has hosted few major tournaments other than the 1930 PGA, the 1951 Ryder Cup, and the 1962 Amateur.

Pinehurst's amateur roots are as strong as any, and Richard Tufts, grandson of the founder, inaugurated the World Amateur Team Championship, which is better known these days as the Eisenhower Trophy.

In 1948, the Pinehurst resort was bought by a large conglomerate, the Club Corporation of America, and while they have developed it, the changes have been painless, with the original charm and character retained. One significant addition that no golfer would object to was made in 1974 when Pinehurst was chosen as the site for the World Golf Hall of Fame. Embraced by pools and fountains, it stands, appropriately enough, in the tranquil pine forest next to the 4th green of No 2, the course described by Ross as the 'fairest test of championship golf I have ever designed.'

From an elevated tee, the 4th at Pinehurst winds gently towards a slightly raised green.

PINE VALLEY

Pine Valley was once described by a grumpy visitor as a '184 acre bunker.' Another, on hearing his friend remark that it was penal, added: 'It is not penal, it is a penitentiary.' One distinguished official took 44 shots to complete a par three, while the club championship has been won with a score of 33 over par. If you want to hear about horror stories and golf, then come to Pine Valley.

From such tales do legends grow of course, and like most legends, this one has been blown out of proportion. The stories give the impression that Pine Valley is unplayable but it is not that. It is above all, the archetypal penal course. That is to say, on almost every hole there is only one route to the green. Diverge only fractionally from the prescribed path and you may be heading for a triple-bogey. A brute perhaps, but one that rewards the player not intimidated by the omnipresent pine trees and sand. Peter McEvoy and Peter Baker were five under par for 16 holes of a foursome match during the 1985 Walker Cup. While another leading amateur, Woody Platt, played the first four holes in six under par. Mind you, he knew that could not last. He promptly left the course at that point and retired to the bar before real life could intrude.

No course is more daunting than Pine Valley and one of the reasons is clear from this photograph taken from the tee at the par-three 14th.

Philadelphia Story

The creation of Pine Valley is an extraordinary story of the dedication of one man, a Philadelphia hotelier by the name of George A Crump. On first seeing the site, Crump declared it a golf course just waiting to be born, and from that day gave up the good life, and committed his soul to doing justice to the land. He even built a bungalow on site so he could spend not only his waking hours there but his sleeping ones as well. Over the next five years, he literally hacked out one of America's great courses. He spent $250,000 of his own money with little thought of repayment, and when he died, with 14 holes completed, he made sure there was enough in his estate to complete the masterpiece. At least before he died he had earned the praise of his peers for a golf course of singular beauty. Donald Ross, of Pinehurst and Dornoch fame, went so far as to declare it the best golf course in America.

With pine hugging virtually every fairway this is no course for spectators and the club have never sought professional events. Two Walker Cups have been held there though, both ending in victory for the Americans.

'Watch it, watch it,' the British Amateur Laddie Lucas instructed his caddie during the 1936 Walker Cup match as a sliced drive headed for the jungle. 'You don't have to watch 'em here,' the caddie replied. 'Just listen for 'em.'

With two par-fives that no-one has ever reached in two shots and with intimidating short holes that offer safe havens only on the tees and greens and absolutely nowhere in between, no wonder Pine Valley's members have a standing bet that no-one breaks 80 at their first attempt.

One man who did was Arnold Palmer, in 1954, when he was Amateur champion. Years later, Palmer would recall a very special round. 'I was broke at the time,' he said. 'So I collected all the bets I could find. I don't know what I would have done if I had lost – it was far more money than I could afford. But everything turned out all right.' Armed with a 68 at Pine Valley things would continue to work out for Palmer.

At the 5th there's a belt of scrub, a two-tier green, bunkers and a creek. No wonder the locals say: 'Only God can make a three here.'

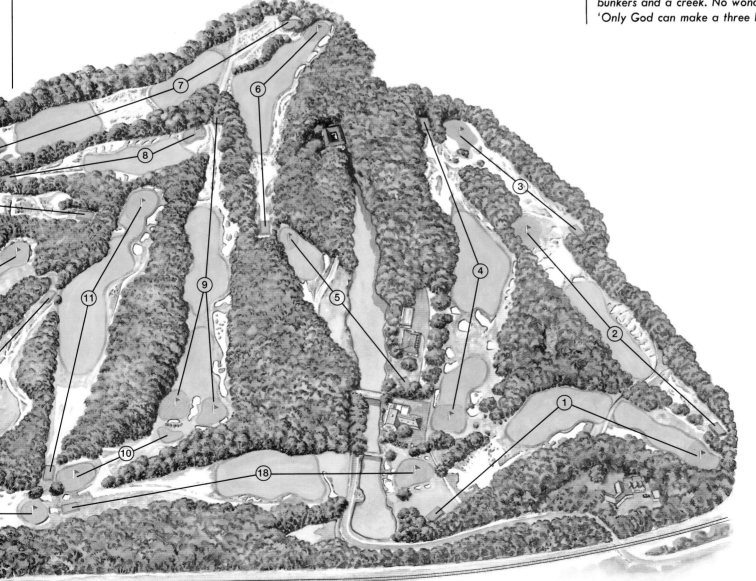

PORTMARNOCK

Ireland is blessed with a number of links courses that stand comparison with the finest that Scotland has to offer. And of all the emerald island's links, perhaps the finest of all is Portmarnock. Jutting out on a peninsula some eight miles north-east of the fair city of Dublin, Portmarnock is surrounded by sea on three sides, and while it boasts neither the vast dunes of Ballybunion to the west, nor the magical tranquillity of Killarney in the southwest, it offers links golf at its most authentic.

Like all the best links courses, Portmarnock's design is natural rather than contrived. The chances of a good score are dictated not only by the quality of the player but by how he copes with the different climatic conditions. And how they differ! In the teeth of a tempest in the 1927 Irish Open, only

one man, George Duncan, went round in less than 80. Contrast that with Bernhard Langer's sublime performance in 1987, when he gave one of the finest displays of 72-hole golf seen in recent European Tour history. In ideal weather, Langer shot 67-68-66-68, and the full measure of his achievement is shown by the fact that the runner-up, Sandy Lyle, was no less than 10 shots adrift.

Play over 18 holes at Portmarnock commenced in 1899, when they also had their first professional tournament. The winner could hardly have been more appropriate for a course destined for greatness, for it was none

---

A short pilgrimage from Dublin and the golfer arrives at Portmarnock, home for many years of the Irish Open and the scene of the 1990 Walker Cup match.

other than Harry Vardon, who later that year would win the third of his six British Open titles.

In 1991, Portmarnock will have one of its proudest occasions when the top amateurs from Great Britain and Ireland defend the Walker Cup against their American counterparts.

Over the years, changes have been made and greens redesigned, but perhaps the biggest is the fact you no longer have to get to the club by boat. Such was the case in the early years and a perilous journey it was, if legend is to be believed. For it is said the club ferryman was a formidable character, and once there was a difference of opinion between himself and a clergyman not of the same faith. The clergyman did not reach Portmarnock. These days, such is the quality of Irish hospitality, the problem is tearing yourself away.

ROYAL BIRKDALE

*I*t is a curious fact that two of the best British courses both celebrated their centenary in the same year. In Northern Ireland in 1989 the toast was to Royal County Down, in England to the fair links at Royal Birkdale – 'fair' in this context to mean both beautiful and equitable. All too often links golf depends too much on the run of the ball. Birkdale shows that you can have your cake and eat it too. Here, if your ball is heading in the direction of the rough, that is where it will finish. There's no guarantee you will find it, either: the local willow scrub is among the most penal in the land.

Birkdale is one of the jewels in the English golfing crown. It really is the most remarkable stretch of land to be found in the country. Drive around this area and all you can see are golf courses, or golf courses waiting to be built. Stare out over the many untouched dunes that line this stretch of coastland just south of Southport and you could design a course yourself. Neighboring Birkdale, for example, is Hillside, a course good enough to host a British PGA and an Amateur Championship; and many rate it alongside big brother next door. But Birkdale fully deserves its premier position.

Substantially re-designed in 1954 it is widely held to be, with Muirfield, the best and fairest of the British Open Championship venues. It has held the event six times, and in addition there have been two Ryder Cup matches, one Walker Cup, one Curtis Cup, British and English Championships, plus various events on the European Tour.

The oldest golf cliché is that a course is only as good as the champions it produces, and Birkdale scores highly in this respect as well. Peter Thomson and Tom Watson, the two most successful players in the modern Open era, both scored their fifth Championship victories there. Together with Arnold Palmer, Lee Trevino and Johnny Miller they make a formidable circle of winners indeed. And between them, the quintet have produced some truly unforgettable moments.

The Palmer Plaque

The one that lingers most of all is from during Palmer's year in 1961. At the 15th (now the 16th) he drove wildly

into the scrub and contemplated an impossible-looking shot. The sensible option was to play for the fairway; but the Welshman Dai Rees was breathing down Palmer's neck and he knew that if his advantage was to be retained, he would have to go for it. The trouble was that the green, assuming he could somehow propel the ball that far, was protected by two cavernous bunkers. Palmer advanced it 160 yards with his 6-iron, the ball coming to rest 16ft from the pin. He uprooted a tree in the process – and shook Rees to the very core as well. In the end the difference between them was the one shot that Palmer had saved on that hole. To commemorate a miraculous blow, a plaque was erected that still stands on the side of this fairway.

Watson made one of his greatest shots at Birkdale as well. This came at the 18th, which is sometimes played as a par-five but in this British Open, was

It was a spot from which many spectators thought Palmer would be lucky to make contact with the ball but instead he found the green.

a mean four of 472 yards. Watson required par for victory, but even after the perfect drive (no small feat with all sorts of peril awaiting any man on the right) he still had over 200 yards to the green. With the crowd converging all around him, Watson took out his 2-iron and played what he later described as a shot that would stay with him for the rest of his life. It flew unerringly towards its target, and with that shot the British Open was won.

Seve Takes a Bow

If Birkdale has given us great winners it has also introduced us to prospective champions as well. In the 1976 British Open there emerged a Spaniard by the

name of Ballesteros. The precocious 18-year-old's opening drive of the Championship shall always be remembered. The conventional wisdom when playing this hole is to take a long iron so as not to dabble with a dune that juts out sharply from the left. Ballesteros did not dabble with it, but then neither did he take out an iron. Using his driver, he deployed all his might to smash a shot right over the corner.

That year all were taking afternoon siestas as the sun blazed all week and temperatures touched the nineties. Ballesteros was quite at home, and it was at Birkdale that he made Britain his second home. He played the first 36 holes in 69, 69, and when he recognized that experience in the form of

The 12th hole at Royal Birkdale is one of the finest short holes in the world. Pinpoint accuracy is required to thread the ball past the many and various hazards that lie in wait for the timid golfer.

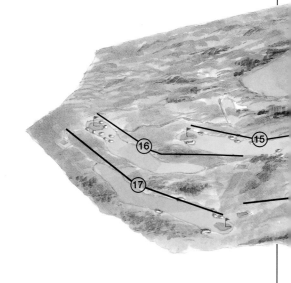

Miller had beaten him on the final day, there were smiles all round. Would that all sports were like that.

One of Golf's Gentlemen

Would that all sports, too, could copy the final moments of the 1969 Ryder Cup at Birkdale, which contained one of golf's most famous acts of sportsmanship. As Jack Nicklaus and Tony

Jacklin made their way to the final green of the final singles match, they were all square, with the match as a whole similarly poised. Nicklaus's birdie putt finished some 4ft past the hole, Jacklin's half that length. The Golden Bear nervelessly holed his, leaving Jacklin knowing that if he missed, the glory of his British Open victory (earned just 20 miles away two months earlier) would be dimmed. He would be remembered as the man who missed the shortest putt to lose the Ryder Cup. Such momentous thoughts clouded his mind but then Nicklaus relieved him of them. He conceded the putt, and sealed a Birkdale legend.

Perhaps the most talked about hole on the course is the par-three 12th. Although it is no great length – less than 190 yards – it always calls for a long iron, and invariably there is a wind just aching to pull your ball off line. The target is a small green that looks miles away from the back tee. It is like threading the ball through the eye of a needle. It is a classic Birkdale hole with the green heavily protected on all sides by the omnipresent dunes. This is the essence of the course. Hit a shot flush and true and your reward will be the middle of the fairway or the middle of the green. But stray by much on either side and all sorts of peril awaits. On the one hand they recognize that if they play badly they will be treated so. On the other, glory awaits the shotmaker whose day has come.

The 13th can be played either as a short par-five or a long par-four but the straight hitter has nothing to fear.

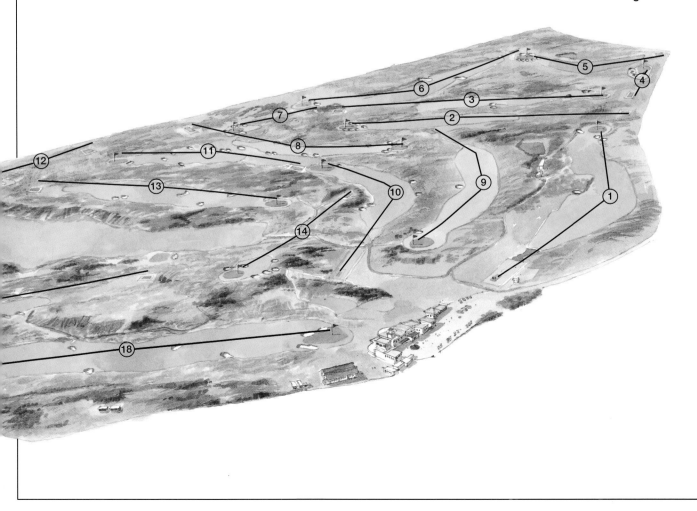

ROYAL CALCUTTA

oyal Calcutta is the oldest golf club in the world outside the British Isles, and an extravagant reminder of the sumptuous days of the Raj. Founded in 1829 as the Dum-Dum Club (after Calcutta's north-eastern suburb), it later moved further south to leafier Tollygunge. The name Royal Calcutta befits a place with the grandest of clubhouses and a course that is never in anything less than immaculate condition. It stands like a colossus over Indian golf and is immensely proud of its strong links with the Royal and Ancient which stretch back to the days of its birth, for there is some evidence that Scots were involved. Until recently the club

was even the governing body in India, and every year a silver tankard donated by the R&A is one of the most prized club competitions.

In addition to its pioneering status, Royal Calcutta was also the first course to demonstrate that golf could be played in the tropics on grass and not sand. The local dhoob grass proved ideal, and since then dhoob and related grasses have become the norm for courses in all but the temperate zones.

The most conspicuous obstacles on the course are the innumerable tanks (ponds and lakes) used to store water. They also serve as swimming pools for local boys and girls who will save your

ball from a watery grave provided you pay them a few coins in return. The local women do their washing in the tanks – a reminder that Royal Calcutta is an oasis of opulence in a city of semi-starving millions.

One of the feature holes is the 7th, a tortuous par four of some 457 yards, with carries over water from the tee and from the approach. Its notoriety has spread throughout India and many a player has stepped on to this tee and been intimidated into fluffing his drive. Other first class holes are the par-three 2nd and 13th which can play from 230 yards down to 150: here, too, water threatens any ball that departs from the strictest accuracy.

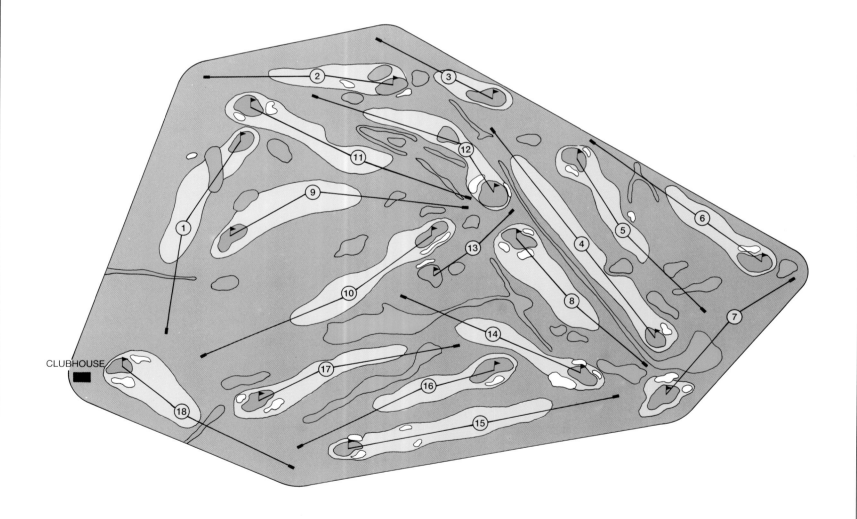

ROYAL COUNTY DOWN

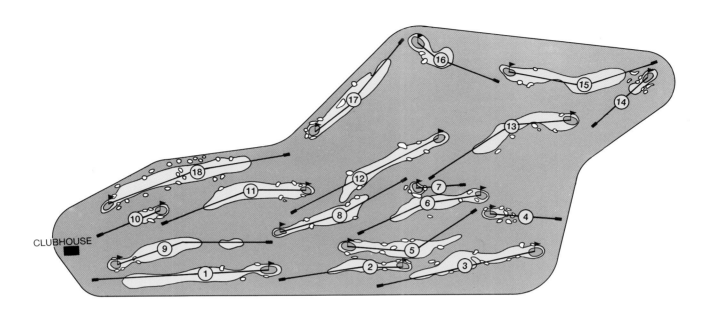

CLUBHOUSE

Where the Mountains of Mourne sweep down to the sea is where you will find Royal County Down, a course the equal in aesthetic appeal of any in the British Isles. It is situated in the small town of Newcastle in Northern Ireland – a location sufficient to render it virtually unplayed for all but the busiest days of the year. The loss is that of the people who think (wrongly) that making the trip would be some sort of security risk.

Certainly to stand on the 1st tee on a clear spring day is to be as far from the troubles in the province – indeed, any troubles at all – as is imaginable. The mountains to your left, complemented by the town spires, invite comparisons with an alpine village, but the glistening sea to your right interrupts this train of thought. In front of you are oceans of yellow gorse and fairways of emerald green. First impressions are often misleading, but not in this instance. The golfer knows instantly that he is about to embark on a memorable journey.

Pedants will insist that any course that features five 'blind' tee shots and a number of similar approach shots could hardly be considered a classic golf course; this criticism of County Down is about as sensible as reproaching Muirfield for an absence of trees: they are part and parcel of the course's character.

Royal County Down, and indeed Newcastle itself, is one of those rare

places that make you feel good simply to be alive. The one British Amateur Championship to have been played there was in 1970, when Michael Bonallack won for a third successive year. Extraordinarily, and without prece-

---

The 10th at Royal County Down, one of three par-threes that run to more than 200 yards. This one runs away from the clubhouse to a green that is only 27 yards in depth.

dent, the man he defeated in the final, Bill Hyndman, had also been runner-up to Bonallack the previous year at Hoylake.

In 1927 the Ladies' British Open Amateur Championship was won by a tiny French lady called Simone Thion de la Chaume, later to become the wife of the legendary tennis player, René Lacoste. (Oddly enough, their daughter, Catherine, also won the event in Northern Ireland, at Portrush.)

ROYAL MELBOURNE

There are some who consider Royal Melbourne to be Dr Alister Mackenzie's finest achievement and compliments come no greater than that. After all we are talking about a man who numbers Augusta National and Cypress Point among his many startling creations. There is little question that a composite of six holes of the East Course designed by his protegé Alex Russell and 12 of the West (Mackenzie's own) creates one of the most complete venues to be found anywhere. No less players than Ben Crenshaw and Greg Norman rate it the finest golf course, full stop.

Ironically, it was somewhat by accident that this composite was hit upon. Chiefly it was an act of expediency, the organizers of the 1959 Canada Cup (now the World Cup) wanted a course that avoided the busy roads that cross both the East and the West. This com-

The Melbourne greens, like those at Augusta, are mesmerizingly quick. A heavy hand on the putter can prove very costly on these glassy surfaces as many have discovered.

posite combines all the traits that have become the hallmark of the Mackenzie championship courses. Melbourne is a myriad of large, aesthetically pleasing bunkers, and severely contoured, wonderfully conditioned greens. Like Augusta, the latter are mesmerizingly quick, and like Augusta it is not a question of just hitting the greens with your second shot, but rather, placing them precisely in terms of where the holes are cut.

Like Cypress Point, there is a short par-four that is the essence of temptation. Once more it falls in the middle of the round. At Cypress it is the 9th, here the 8th. The green is 300 yards away, and many a professional has stood on this tee and dreamed his dream of an eagle two. But a two requires the perfect tee shot over an enormous bunker that guards the approach to the green. Anything less than a perfect shot along this line is likely to spell disaster.

But the toughest par-four on this course is surely the 470-yard 14th, where a blind drive over massive fairway bunkers is followed by a long iron from a sloping fairway to a large green haunted by subtle borrows and guarded on the line of approach by three more bunkers. This is a hole where a par brings all the satisfaction of a birdie. Set to win the event, Supermex ran up a nine. The 15th, too, is a card wrecker as Bruce Crampton discovered in the 1972 World Cup. Just as he and Bill Dunk looked to have the event won for the host nation, he stumbled to an extremely costly double-bogey six.

The Great Gold Rush

Golf began in Melbourne in the 1840s but it was not until the discovery of gold in New South Wales that the game reached a proper footing. Organized golf was revived in 1891 and royal patronage was approved four years later, following a request from the Earl of Hopetoun, Governor of Victoria.

As the premier course in Australia, Royal Melbourne has hosted all that is worth staging in the Southern Hemisphere. In addition to 1959 and 1972, the World Cup has been back on one more occasion, in 1988, when Australia's Roger Mackay established a new course record with a startling 63. But the event was still won by the Ameri-

can team of Ben Crenshaw and Mark McCumber. The World Amateur Team Championship has also visited these parts and again it brought a victory for the United States in a close finish with Great Britain and Ireland.

Royal Melbourne has seen the best

and worst of times. It has witnessed the aforementioned 63, while at the other end of the scale, Sam Surrudhin of Indonesia came limping into the scorer's tent having taken 105. As someone once wrote: it is a course to humble the giants or confirm their greatness.

Top: The dog-leg at the daunting 6th hole on the West course. The angle is heavily protected by bunkers and scrub and the second shot is no easy one either. Right: The closing par-three on Melbourne's East course has a green heavily protected by sand.

ROYAL MONTREAL

Royal Montreal, like a great many other clubs formed during golf's pioneering days, originated when a group of Scots got together to re-create their national sport on foreign soil. This particular gathering, centered around the patriarchal figure of Alexander Dennistoun, a man with Royal connections who formed the oldest club in North America and one that has substantially contributed to the way the game is played in Canada. Members of the club founded the Royal Canadian Golf Association and the club's annual match against The Country Club of Brookline, Massachusetts, was the first international encounter between clubs from two different countries. Furthermore, they initiated the first national championships, the women's and men's amateur events, plus the inaugural Canadian Open.

The first layout was on land purchased in a park surrounding the cliff of Mount Royal that gave the city its name. The Royal decree followed from Queen Victoria in 1884, but regal patronage was no compensation for the fact that the holes kept changing their positions in the park. It was not long before it became obvious that the site was unsuitable.

In 1896 the club bought enough land 10 miles out of the city to lay two fine golf courses, with transport provided by the Canadian National Railways, or Canadian Pacific as it then was, which ran parallel. The courses were excellent but once again the demands of the city proved great and as the huge Montreal international airport went up, so the golf club moved out.

The Lake of Two Mountains

This time they chose the rural calm of a small island known as Ile Bizard, which is 10 miles further out from the city center. Dick Wilson was flown up from Florida to orchestrate work on the new courses, and his qualifications as a civil engineer proved useful for there

was all manner of rocks to move, and swampland to be drained from the site located in the Lake of Two Mountains.

The courses were opened in 1959 and Wilson was proud of his creation. He said: 'There is a sweep and dimension to this layout which can only be de-scribed as exciting. The vista of the Lake of Two Mountains is the perfect backdrop to these courses.'

It took Wilson just two years to create this new course and the members were well pleased. At a stroke the roar of jet engines vanished, and the burgeoning road and rail traffic was a thing of the past, while there was some excellent golf to be had on both the Blue and the Red courses. Every hole lives up to Wilson's philosophy that a golf hole should represent a hard par but an easy bogey, and it is accepted that a Royal Montreal player can play to his handicap anywhere. The most conspicuous characteristic is the huge greens, which in one case

The 13th hole on the Red course exhibits the beautifully manicured but demanding features typical of the course as a whole.

measures 140ft from tip to toe, while water comes into play on each of the closing holes.

During the 1975 Canadian Open, an intense young professional called Pat Fitzsimmons hooked his drive at the feared 16th, and was about to give it up as being in the water. Just as he prepared to reload, he was informed that it had landed on a hitherto unknown is-

land about the size of a raft. There was no obvious way to get to the perfectly playable ball, other than that which Fitzsimmons eventually chose. He waded out in waist-deep water to the island, from where he hit an excellent 4-iron to the green and after partially drying himself, he two putted for his par. And the inconsequential island has been named Fitzsimmons Island.

A spectacular aerial view of the 15th (left) and the 16th (right) on the Blue course where water provides the main threat.

ST. ANDREWS

'There are those who do not like the golf at St. Andrews, and they will no doubt deny any charm to the links themselves, but there must surely be none who will deny a charm to the place as a whole. It may be immoral, but it is delightful to see a whole town given up to golf; to see the butcher and the baker and the candlestick maker shouldering their clubs as soon as his day's work is done and making a dash for the links. There he and his fellows will very possibly get in our way, or we shall get in theirs; we shall often curse the crowd and wish wholeheartedly that golf was less popular at St. Andrews. Nevertheless it is that utter self-abandonment to golf that gives the place its attractiveness.'

Thus did the that most literary of golf writers, Bernard Darwin begin a passage about St. Andrews in 1910 and the words ring as true today as they did then. It is quite simply, the home of golf, and while the butcher and the candlestick maker have been replaced

The course, and the beach, in a photo where time stands still for it could not have looked much different to this 500 years ago.

The 1989 British Open Champion Mark Calcavecchia plays out of a deep greenside bunker at the 17th during the 1990 competition.

by the building society and the bank, the 'old grey toun' retains its aura as a shrine to the sport they call the royal and ancient game.

The Mecca of Golf

Pilgrims come from all over the world to worship and now it is not the townsfolk who throng the fairways Japanese and Americans and the newly golf-obsessed from the continent of Europe. But still the place retains its special atmosphere. The intimacy of the town, which boasts the oldest university in Scotland, and the feeling of walking on a course that has played host to one sport for well over 400 years add up to a unique golfing experience.

Golf bores, bereft of romance, will insist that the sport had its origins at places other than St. Andrews, but while all that remains uncertain, what we do know is that there has been play on the Old Course since at least 25 January 1552. Then the dignitaries of the town granted the public the right to use the links to 'play at golf, futball, schuteing...with all other manner of pastimes.' The proprietor was bound

'not to plough up any part of said golf links in all time coming' but to reserve them for the comfort and amusement of the inhabitants. And so it has followed that for more than 400 years, every golfer has enjoyed a right to play over the course, and only within the present century has a green fee been imposed.

Natural Evolution

The Old Course has never known an architect, owing more to the whims of nature than the hand of man. The evidence is everywhere; there are no less than 14 par-four holes, and the layout has remained unchanged ever since the Royal and Ancient Club was formed in 1754. And as far as most people are concerned it has stood the test of time. First impressions would find most people agreeing with Sam Snead, that the course 'ain't worth a dime.' Most change their tune upon repeated exposure, and none more so than the immortal Bobby Jones, whose love of the place was matched only by the respect and affection returned by the St. Andrews people. Jones tore up his card at the short 11th the first time he encountered the Old Course in the British

Open of 1921, but his feeling of shame at his behavior at St. Andrews, of all places, had a profound effect on Jones and on his future conduct as a golfer. He later returned to St. Andrews to win the British Open (1927) and the British Amateur Championship (1930). And when he was given the freedom of St. Andrews in 1958, he delighted his audience with the words: 'I could take out of my life everything except my experiences at St. Andrews and still have had a rich, full life.'

The Old Course is rated pretty highly in the field of golf architecture. The distinguished designer Robert Trent Jones has written: 'The first few rounds a golfer plays on the Old Course are not likely to alter his first estimate that it is vastly overrated. He will be puzzled to understand the rhapsodies that have been composed about the perfect strategic position of its trapping, the subtle undulations of its huge greens, the endless tumbling of its fairways which seldom give him a chance to play a shot

Nowhere is more instantly recognizable than the first and 18th fairways at St Andrews, with the magnificent clubhouse lying beyond.

from a level stance. Then, as he plays on, he begins to realize that whenever he plays a fine shot he is rewarded; whenever he doesn't play the right shot he is penalised in proportion; and whenever he thinks out his round hole by hole he scores well.' Trent Jones's words are a perfect definition of the central precepts of strategic design in golf course architecture.

The layout of the course paved the way for the traditional links design where the first nine holes make their way out from the clubhouse and the second nine bring the golfer back. Most unusually, 14 of the holes are serviced by just seven double-greens. A pulled approach shot at the 2nd hole, for example, could finish on that part of the green around the flag for the 16th hole. Retaining par, however is far from straightforward. Indeed once you contemplate the humps and hollows, not to mention the borrows of a more subtle nature, you may feel you would have been better off missing the green altogether.

Mark Calcavecchia was so bemused by the 'putt' left to him after a poor second shot in the 1989 Dunhill Cup that he (quite legally) used his wedge to the consternation of the traditionalists. The single greens are on the 1st, 9th, 17th and 18th holes.

The opening drive on the Old Course could hardly be easier. Ahead of you lies the expanse of fairways of the 1st and 18th holes, the size of several football fields. The only danger is out of

bounds at right angles to the tee or the Swilcan Burn which falls just short of the green at a driving distance of 350 yards.

The Road Hole

Of all the holes at St. Andrews, the 17th – a par-4 of 461 yards – must be the best-known and most feared. So many championship hopes have come to grief at this, the Road Hole, the visitor can almost hear the sound of gentle weeping and gnashing of teeth as the ghosts of golfers' past welcome him on to the green. The drive requires you to drive over, or fade around, the corner of what once were railroad sheds but are now part of the exceedingly ugly hotel

alongside the 17th fairway. The approach shot is still more perilous. Taking a bite out of the left-front of a shallow green is the Road Hole bunker, a horribly deep and steep-sided abyss, while beyond the green a scrubby bank gives on to a metalled road with a wall behind it.

The most noticeable casualty here in recent years was Tom Watson, the most successful Open champion of the modern era. He was looking to tie Harry Vardon's record of six titles in 1984, but overclubbed his second shot, a 2-iron, sending his ball through the green, over the road, and against the wall. He registered a bogey, Severiano Ballesteros went on to win, and Watson's aura of omnipotence had gone for ever.

Even if you hit the green, such are its contours that peril has still not passed. The flag is invariably cut close to the Road Hole bunker for the British Open's final round, and Englishman Brian Barnes and Japan's Tommy Nakajima are among dozens of players who have hit the green in two only to putt into the sand. Poor Nakajima, in contention for the 1978 Open, needed four shots to get out of the bunker, thereby registering a 10 and endowing this hazard with the name 'the sands of Nakajima'! If the 17th is perilous, the 354-yard closing hole could hardly be more inviting. The player has a fairway 100 yards wide to aim at. The peril

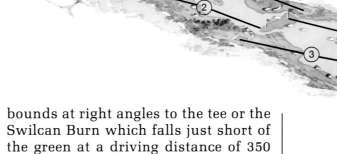

comes with the Valley of Sin, a deceptive depression near the left front of the green. Of course, you avoid the trouble by 'doing a Nicklaus'. In the play-off in 1970, the 'Golden Bear' took off his sweater on the 18th tee and smashed the ball to the back of the green.

In the final round of that British Open, Doug Sanders had missed the shortest putt that ever lost the one of the game's most prestigious trophies.

An aerial view of the 17th vividly demonstrates the difficulty of the tee shot. The second shot is hardly any easier.

Sanders was deceived by one of the 18th green's slyest borrows and allowed Nicklaus to force the playoff.

Nicklaus, like, Jones, is a golfer held in as much affection as esteem by the people of St. Andrews; and he, again like Jones, has been made an Honorary Burgess of the city. The only other American upon whom this distinction has been conferred was the great 18th-century scientist and statesman Benjamin Franklin. The old city certainly knows how to pick them.

SEMINOLE

They seem to build golf courses at the rate of one an hour these days in Florida. But, while some of the modern ones are beauties, like Grand Cypress, Genelefe and Lake Nona to name but three in Orlando alone – the all-important and hard-to-replicate quality of tradition means that people still fall back on the golden oldies like Seminole.

Situated on the east coast 15 miles north of Palm Beach, Seminole is a prime example of the work of the Scottish architect Donald Ross. He designed hundreds of courses all over the States but it is said that the site on which Seminole rests was the only one he sought; for the rest he was commissioned. He was given some classic raw materials with which to work. Indeed, with the ocean backdrop and the fine springy turf, together with the warm sea breezes and swaying palm trees, the area combines all the best of the Old World, whence Ross came, with the New where he made his home and fortune. Ben Hogan once said: 'If you can play well there, you can play well anywhere,' and he picked out the 390-yard 6th as the best par-four in the world. This is the most dramatic of holes with all manner of strategically placed bunkers. One can understand its appeal to Hogan: it requires strength of will as well as consummate shot-making to make par.

Seminole is a thinking man's course with far greater demands made on accuracy and wit than on strength. Avoiding the bunkers is no easy task: there are over 200 of them. Nevertheless, for the talented player whose day has come, Seminole will yield. The resident professional there for many years was the 1948 Masters champion Claude Harmon, and he once went round in just 60 strokes. A map of his remarkable achievement hangs on the clubhouse wall.

Seminole, built in 1920, is one of the wealthiest and most exclusive clubs in the United States. Its members have the good fortune to play on the country's finest course south of Augusta National.

Situated on a prime piece of Florida coastline Seminole's trademark is vast swathes of sand.

SHINNECOCK HILLS

Excellent though most of them are, there is a uniformity about U.S. Open courses that has evoked valid criticism from people such as Lee Trevino, Tom Watson, Raymond Floyd and just about every European professional. No-one has complained, however, about two glorious exceptions, which are separated by the vast width of the country. One, in California, is Pebble Beach. The other, on Long Island, New York, is Shinnecock Hills.

The admiration in which this pair are held is universal, and no wonder. Each takes golf back to its roots and the days when the only water to be found on courses was spray from a storm-tossed sea on greens placed perilously close to the shore. At Shinnecock, the Atlantic Ocean is visible from the highest points but it is not, strictly, a links course. Rather, the view more resembles Sunningdale in England, as does the texture of the greens and fairways. 'Shinnecock is one of the finest courses I have played,' Ben Hogan said in the 60s. 'Each hole is different and requires a great amount of skill to play properly. You know exactly where to shoot and the distance is easy to read.'

Vanderbilt's Legacy

Shinnecock dates from the last decade of the 19th century. During the winter of 1890–1, William K Vanderbilt, the founder of the Vanderbilt dynasty and a prominent sportsman in his own right, was travelling through France when he came across the Scottish professional Willie Dunn in Biarritz. Dunn was building a course there and gave an impromptu exhibition of his golfing skills. Vanderbilt was enthralled. Instantly he thought of the exciting possibility of importing the game to Southampton on Long Island. So in the summer of 1891 Dunn was brought over to find a suitable location and he settled on some low-lying sandhills that were the site of an ancient Indian burial ground.

U.S. Open venues often attract criticism but this has never been directed at Shinnecock Hills.

With the help of some 150 Indian laborers, Dunn set about work on the first formalized golf course in the United States. He wrote: 'Except for several horse-drawn roadscrapers, all the work was done by hand. The fairways were cleaned off and the natural grass left in. The rough was very rough, with clothes-ripping blueberry bushes, large boulders, and many small gullies. The place was dotted with Indian burial mounds, and we left some of these intact as bunkers in front of the greens. We scraped out some of the mounds, and made sandtraps. It was here that the Indians buried their empty whiskey bottles, but we did not find this out until later, when playing the course. One never knew when an explosion shot in a trap would bring out a couple of firewater flasks, or perhaps a bone or two.'

Thus twelve holes were laid out. Stanford White, the most fashionable architect of the time, was brought in

to design a luxury clubhouse, complete with grill room, shower-baths and lockers. There is no question that Shinnecock was the place to be. Within a year of its opening it had been extended to 18 holes, and in 1894 it was one of the five founder members of the United States Golf Association.

In 1896 Shinnecock was the venue for the second U.S. Open, but instead of this being a celebration of its attributes, rather the limitations of the course were found out. At less than 5,000 yards it clearly was not of championship calibre. It was not until 1931 that the present-day course finally emerged. Largely the work of Dick Wilson, Shinnecock was extended to its present length of 6,697 yards and converted into a full championship test. Wilson designed the course so the shorter par-fours play into the prevailing wind and the longer ones with it. The par-three holes are splendidly varied, too, the pick of them being perhaps the beautiful 17th, which appropriately bears the name of Eden.

But despite all the improvements and amendments, Shinnecock was not deemed worthy to stage another Open.

No-one had any complaints about the layout, but with the nearest cities, New York and Boston, both being a good two hours away, it was thought the event would not attract large enough crowds; and even if it did, it was argued, the hotel accommodation in the immediate area would be inadequate. Finally, the site was thought not large enough to handle all the extraneous facilities that go with the national championship of America.

The Open Returns

Eventually, however, the USGA relented. They decided that on the 90th anniversary of its first staging, the Open would return to Shinnecock Hills. Ben Crenshaw, for one, could hardly believe the good news. 'At the 1986 U.S. Open, the players will have the privilege of playing Shinnecock,' he declared. Raymond Floyd was delighted as well. He disliked even the best of the Open venues. It was a primary reason why this most combative of competitors had never won the event. But the first time he set eyes on Shinnecock he knew he had found a course that made his heart sing.

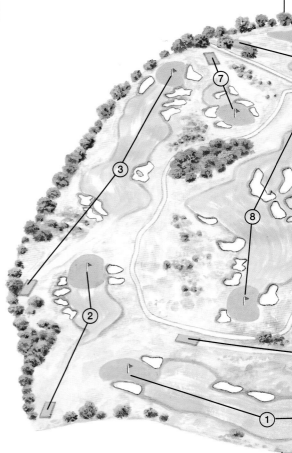

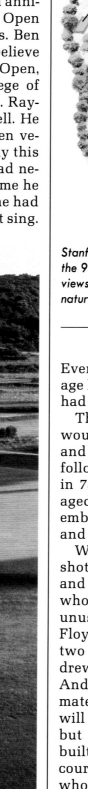

Stanford White's clubhouse (right) overlooks both the 9th and 18th greens (left) and offers excellent views of the surrounding course. There is also a natural grandstand for the home green.

Even though he was 43 and no-one that age had ever won the Open, he knew he had his best chance in years.

The first day brought weather that would have made Scotland quiver, and there was no hint of what was to follow for Floyd as he struggled round in 75 shots. But no-one else had managed to break 70, either, and when the embattled veteran added rounds of 68 and 70, he was in contention.

With six holes to play he was three shots behind the leader Payne Stewart, and the difference between a player who thrives under pressure and one unused to such moments was stark. Floyd, who had won each of the other two major American championships, drew strength from those experiences. And a wonderful last round of 66 ultimately gave him a two-shot victory he will savor not just as Open champion but because it occurred on a course built for great deeds. 'I wish all our courses were like this,' said Trevino, who finished three shots back.

And it is highly appropriate that for its centenary celebrations in 1995 the Open will return to this sublime corner of Long Island.

SOTOGRANDE

*T*here are two courses at this luxurious resort, which lies on the Spanish Costa del Sol, some 22 miles north-east of Gibraltar. Both were designed by the doyen of modern American course designers, Robert Trent Jones. The first, the Old Course, was his first European venture. (Old is a relative term. In this case it means as recent as 1965.) The New, or Valderrama as it is known these days, plays host to the end of season event on the European Tour, the Volvo Masters, and is rated by the players as equal to anything they compete on all year. 'Never mind equal, it is better than any other,' the Irishman Ronan Rafferty said. And that was *before* he won the 1989 event. For all that, it is the Old that still gets most of the plaudits. Both courses betray the hand of an American architect; long tees, big greens, white sand traps and water, water, everywhere.

On the Old, the water makes particular demands on five of the incoming holes and the water freak Jones considered these the best on the course. The 12th is right down the side of a lake. The 13th is so protected by two pieces of water that any errant shot is instantly doomed. The 14th is a tee shot over a lake and how hard you make it depends on your nerve, but the bolder the stroke, the easier the approach, always presuming dry land is found of course.

On the New, the 4th looked a hard enough par-five anyway, but a $1.75 million waterfall was recently add ted by two pieces of water that any errant shot is instantly doomed. The 14th is a tee shot over a lake and how hard you make it depends on your nerve, but the bolder the stroke, the easier the approach, always presuming dry land is found of course.

On the New, the 4th looked a hard enough par-five anyway, but a $1.75 million waterfall was recently addard.'

Fabulous Fairways

As well as the Americanized design, the courses have been conditioned to the highest specifications. Trent Jones decided to go with Bermuda grass, the first time it had been used in Europe, to combat the fierce Mediterranean summers. Two sacks of seed from Georgia proved sufficient for a nursery from

Left: The Valderrama course upon which the last event of the European tour is played each season. As in most Trent Jones designed courses water is a prominent feature on both Valderrama and Sotogrande Old (right).

to combat the fierce Mediterranean summers. Two sacks of seed from Georgia proved sufficient for a nursery from which all the fairways were sown. The results are spectacular. There is no such thing as a bad lie at Sotogrande, well not on the fairways anyway, as an automatic electric system feeds almost 1,000 watering points. Taking a divot almost feels like you are slicing up a bowling green.

Feature holes? On the Old, the 422-yard 7th is where Trent Jones began his water sport and it is probably the most spectacular hole on the course. The drive is into a narrow fairway with out of bounds on the left and a large bunker on the right. The approach is to a green well protected by trees, and which slopes away towards two bunkers and the the lake.

On the New, the aforementioned 4th warrants special attention, while the 12th is a long par-three down an avenue of trees. Designed by an American it may be, but the cork trees that dot both courses are undeniably Spanish as is the wonderful Andalusian vista.

From many holes the view is simply breathtaking and the development of clusters of white villas all over the mountainside enhances rather than detracts. Sotogrande lies just 22 miles from Gibraltar and casts a similarly imposing shadow over golf in the area as does the Rock. Many courses have since been built in the region but for many people the only venue that compares with Sotogrande Old is Valderrama.

SUNNINGDALE

Greg Norman, in a typical flash of optimism, once ventured the thought that with everything going for him he could probably break 60 around Sunningdale's Old Course. After playing its 18 holes, it is unlikely you will feel the same way but you will appreciate the feeling underlying Norman's remark. In the view of many, Sunningdale is Britain's best inland course. It is certainly one of the most beautiful — a venue that makes you feel good. The views are splendid,

the course condition invariably likewise, and if you are in form, Sunningdale will pander to your ego and deliver unto you a good score.

It is, however, no pushover. The opening par-five, at a little under 500 yards, is the gentlest starting hole in all of tournament golf, and the 3rd is a par-four of less than 300 yards. But the par-four 5th represents danger to any scorecard. And so it continues.

Ian Woosnam won the European Open there with a score of 20 under

par; against that Great Britain and Ireland's Walker Cup golfers hardly broke the regulation mark in any round during their hapless 1987 performance. The award of that match was a singular honour for Sunningdale since it was the first time the Walker Cup had been held in Britain on anything other than a links course. It was a due comment on its standing within the game, not to mention the fact that old Mr British Amateur Golf himself, the now sadly deceased Gerald Micklem, was also, in another guise, Mr Sunningdale.

Jones Sets the Standard

Even off the back tees, the course is only a modest 6,500 yards, and in the summer it can play a lot shorter than that. In 1926, in the southern qualify-

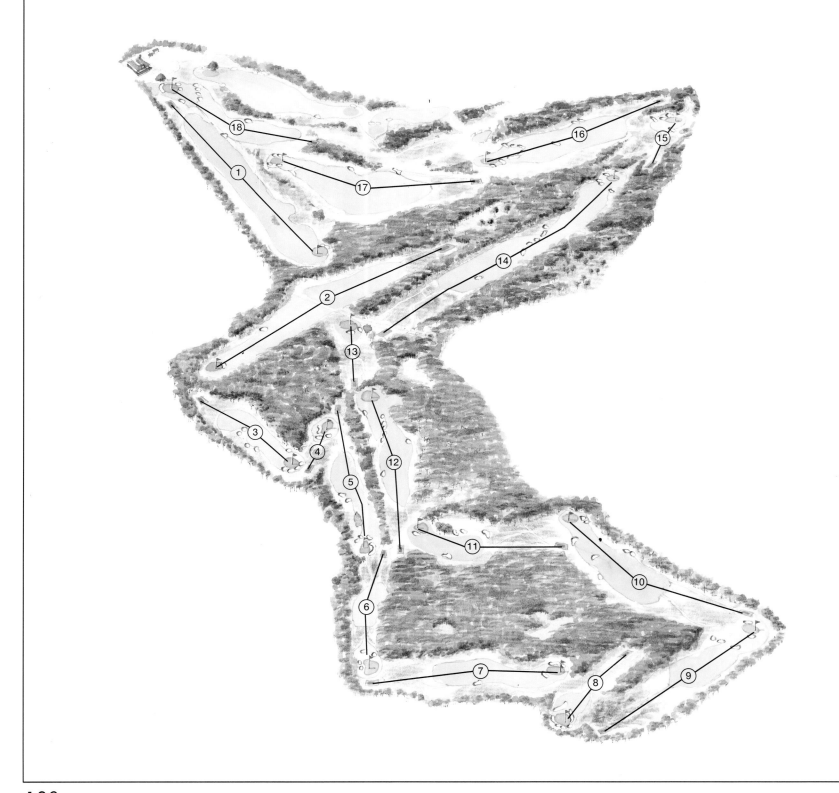

to go round in 74 than 64, and the European Open, which has been played there for seven of the last nine years, has still to produce what might be termed a surprise winner. Far from it indeed, with a roll call that includes Woosnam, Norman, and Langer.

The name Sunningdale suggests something bright and cheerful, something to raise the spirits. The Old Course certainly does that.

Left: The finishing hole and clubhouse at Sunningdale, perhaps the finest inland course in all of Britain. The elevated tee on the 10th hole at Sunningdale (below) offers the golfer an excellent platform from which to view the longest par-four on the course.

ing competition for the Open Championship, Bobby Jones went round in 66, which consisted of 33 strokes and 33 putts. Every hole was scored in three or four. He missed just one green, the 13th, by a matter of a few feet, but he chipped close for his par. Because of its symmetry it became known as the perfect round, although times (and equipment) have so changed it could hardly be regarded in such a light today. The course record, held by Nick Faldo, is now four shots lower. And these days any professional who took 33 putts on Sunningdale's subtle but inviting greens would certainly feel he ought to put in a bit of overtime on the practice green. Perhaps the most vivid illustration of how scoring has improved, however, came in 1988 with Woosnam's victory when he averaged scores of one better in each round than Jones's 66.

Jones however, was sold on the place. The man who later created Augusta National added a 68 in the second qualifying round and said: 'I wish I could take this place home with me.' The course was laid out at the start of the century by Willie Park, Jr, who had won two British Open championships in the 1880s. Later the noted architect Harry Colt, who was also secretary at Sunningdale for 17 years and planted hundreds of trees, made some changes to protect it from the longer flight of the new rubber-cored Haskell ball.

The result was a masterpiece of variety and design. And while no-one would pretend that it is is the stiffest challenge the top professionals meet during the course of a season, it presents a stiff challenge to all but the greatest players. It remains far easier

THE COUNTRY CLUB

The United States is knee-deep in 'country clubs'; but place the definite article before the words and every golfer knows which one you mean. The Country Club is 130 years old and was the first of its kind. It is situated in Brookline, now part of Boston, Massachusetts, and it was the forerunner for the kind of set-up in which thousands of Americans like to play their golf: a condo at the back of the 5th green; tennis courts adjacent to but discreetly hidden from the putting green; card games in a locker room built to house a small army. And yet, while all Americans will recognize these characteristics, the Country Club is actually very English in its setting. Vast elms line the Estate. Close your eyes and think of deepest Berkshire. Gary Player once described it as being 'more English than most English courses.' And again, very English, it is saturated in history. The first

Open played there was the most famous of them all. That was in 1913 when a young Bostonian amateur, Francis Ouimet, triumphed after a play-off against two British players, Ted Ray and the great Harry Vardon. The shots that Ouimet played became known as the shots heard around the world for they signalled the rise of American golf and the end of British dominance. Seventy-five years on at Brookline another British player, Nick Faldo, would again be defeated in a play-off, this time by Curtis Strange.

When The Country Club opened in 1860, it was horses that occupied the members' leisure time, for racing or playing polo. It was 30 years before six golf holes were laid, but that was enough at the time to establish it as one of the five original clubs of the United States Golf Association. The club's match with Royal Montreal, first played in 1898, was the world's

first golf match played between teams of different countries.

Like every course steeped in tradition it has its share of legendary landmarks and most are to be found on the back nine. A score, then, has to be made on the outward half, for after the 9th comes a stretch of four par-four holes that in difficulty and relentless length test the greatest golfers in the world.

Deadly Eleventh

The 11th is the most dangerous hole on the course. With its sharp dog-leg left, a premium drive down the right will leave a 4-iron to a green protected by a pond, bunkers left and right, trees, bushes, and large boulders behind. It is possible to run up any score here and in the 1963 U.S. Open, Arnold Palmer did: he played it in 7-7-6-4 and it cost him the title. Typically, when asked about the hole afterwards, he

One of the oldest courses in the USA, Brookline boasts a huge and luxurious clubhouse.

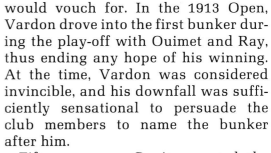

Most holes at Brookline are fringed with thick clusters of trees ready to punish the golfer who strays off line.

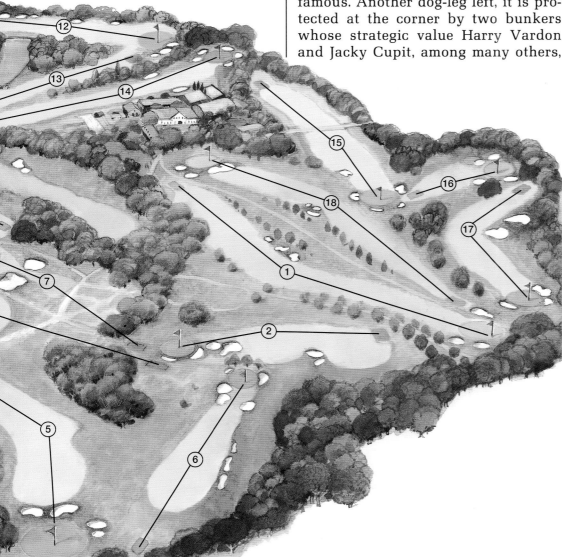

bore it no malice, naming it as one of the best 18 in America.

If the 11th hole is the most arduous, the 17th is undoubtedly the most famous. Another dog-leg left, it is protected at the corner by two bunkers whose strategic value Harry Vardon and Jacky Cupit, among many others, would vouch for. In the 1913 Open, Vardon drove into the first bunker during the play-off with Ouimet and Ray, thus ending any hope of his winning. At the time, Vardon was considered invincible, and his downfall was sufficiently sensational to persuade the club members to name the bunker after him.

Fifty years on, Cupit repeated the trick when two strokes in front. A double-bogey six was the result and he fell back into a play-off, which he lost to Julius Boros.

As befits a course of such standing, other tournaments within the purview of the USGA have been held at the club. It has hosted the Amateur Championship five times – more than any other course – while the Walker Cup has been held there on two occasions. In 1932 the latter match was played during a total eclipse of the sun. But for Leonard Crawley, there might have been a total eclipse of the British team. He was the only visiting player to win a match, but the biggest dent he made was to the cup itself. On the final singles day he misjudged his second shot to the 18th, choosing a 5-iron which sailed over the green and crashed without bouncing into the trophy, causing a dent. Crawley had left his mark, but sadly it was later erased. Crawley was to write: 'I have never forgiven the man who had my dent removed during the long years of the cup's sojourn at St. Andrews during World War II.'

THE JOCKEY CLUB

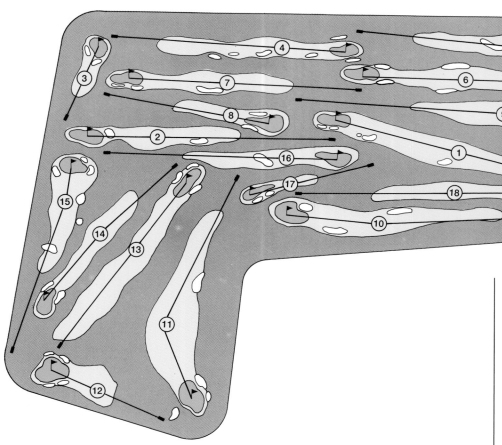

CLUBHOUSE

In designing Royal Melbourne, Augusta National, and Cypress Point, Dr Alister Mackenzie demonstrated that he could do justice to the finest raw materials. The Red Course at the Jockey Club, in Buenos Aires, Argentina, presented a different set of problems altogether. That he succeeded in building perhaps the finest course in South America is a tribute to the skills of a master craftsman.

With more than 100 courses, Argentina boasts more than any other country on that continent, but the name of the club hints at the place golf holds in the sporting scheme of things. In short, golf is a game for the elite, and at the Jockey Club the course was built merely as an additional attraction to horse racing and polo. For all that, Mackenzie took to his task with great gusto, creating mounds here, raising greens there, although sadly he was not to see the opening of the club in 1935. He died a year earlier.

The fruits of his work are such that twice the World Cup has been staged at the Jockey Club. In 1962, the awesomely strong American team of Sam Snead and Arnold Palmer triumphed, but it was the local hero Roberto de Vicenzo who won the individual title. And when the tournament returned in 1970, once more de Vicenzo won the solo honors (Australia took the team prize). Born of a poor family in the city, de Vicenzo had risen to be a hero among the rich and wealthy of the Jockey Club. The key to his success in 1970 was the 10th hole, a typical Mackenzie design where the ability to think clearly brings its rewards. A short par-five of 469 yards, it is a dog-leg to the right, a sharp one, with a massive bunker on the turn. The sensible line therefore would appear to be to play to the left, but the more courageous you are in firing down the middle to right-hand side of the fairway, the better will be your line to the green, since a bunker protects its left hand side. The significance of the 10th was apparent to de Vicenzo, for while his winning margin over Australia's David Graham was just one stroke, he crucially birdied the 10th in every round.

Roberto de Vicenzo twice took the individual honors when the World Cup was staged at his home course in Buenos Aires.

TOURNAMENT PLAYERS' CLUB

The Tournament Players' Club at Sawgrass, Florida was a pioneer, a forerunner of the stadium golf courses that now dot the United States. Many believe it is still the best of the genre. Like all innovations, it also has many critics, one writer alleging on its opening: 'There are enough bad lies to blow the circuits of a polygraph.' The 18th runs alongside a lake, and when Jerry Pate won there one year he threw the architect Pete

Ability to hold the ball on the green can be all important at the TPC – at the 17th especially!

Dye and the Tour commissioner Deane Beman into it. The head of a Florida 'gator is sometimes to be seen in this particular stretch of water and one or two professionals hoped one might make an appearance.

To be fair to Dye, he has listened to more reasoned argument and acted upon it. When the course was first opened it was clear that some of the slopes on the greens were so severe as to be blatantly unfair. So Dye flattened them to the extent that now they are merely perilous.

Dye's original brief was to take into account the improvement in standards, and the improvement in golf equipment, and build a golf course that could test the greatest tournament pros to the utmost. His response was a course that contains 77 greenside bunkers and is veined and dotted with streams and lakes. On the par-three 17th the green is an island entirely surrounded by water except for a narrow access causeway. Here the criticism has run along the lines that there is no margin for error. In fact there is: the green is wide enough, so that if a ball hit by a professional lands in the water it can only come from a careless or over-bold shot.

Cut from Florida swampland, the whole area, some 20 miles from Jacksonville, is now infested with golf clubs, but the Tournament Players' Club remains the most talked about. It is the home each year of The Players' Championship which the U.S. tour has suggested is the fifth major championship. That it is a first class event which attracts most of the finest players in the world is beyond dispute.

TURNBERRY

The sublime ocean setting of Pebble Beach and Cypress Point in California is without equal, but a balmy summer's evening (admittedly not the commonest occurrence) on the Ailsa course at Turnberry runs it close enough for most people. Situated 17 miles south of Ayr, on the Firth of Clyde, on Scotland's west coast, it is the most glamorous of British Open Championship venues, and its holes along the shore have earned it worldwide acclaim.

The 9th hole has the most photographed championship tee in golf, and certainly there is no better starting point on earth upon which to contemplate the drive that follows. The tee sits on a little promontory, some 50 feet above the waves, that points, finger-like towards the vast bulk of Ailsa Craig that rears out of the sea 12 miles to the south-west. To its left is Turnberry's lighthouse; in front there is a carry of 200 yards across a rocky inlet to the fairway beyond, where a marker stone suggests a suitable line for the tee shot.

The Ailsa has hosted only two British Opens, but the first, in 1977, is now widely acknowledged to be the most

exciting of all time, when Jack Nicklaus and Tom Watson, the two greatest players of the day, indulged in a foot race that left the rest of the competitors so breathless that third-placed Hubert Green later remarked: 'Tom won the Open from Jack; I won the

A bird's eye view of the 9th hole at Turnberry. Golfers prone to hook the ball are advised to adopt an open stance.

tournament the rest of us were playing in.' Nine years later, when the British Open returned, the weather was completely different from the mainly idyllic days of 1977. The wind blew and the rain poured. Moreover, the course had been set up altogether more formidably, to prevent any scores like that of Mark Hayes, who had shot 63 in that first Turnberry British Open. But when Greg Norman is firing on all cylinders, not even Turnberry swathed in all that protection can stop him. While many competitors in the second round struggled to score below the mid-70s, Norman matched Hayes's round of 63. Watson hailed it: 'The finest round in any event in which I have been a competitor.'

Anyone passing the course at the end of World War II would have doubted any rounds could have been played at all, fine ones or not. Turnberry was commandeered, as it had been in 1914, to help with the war effort and it needed a vast effort in moving concrete and sand to restore it to eminence. It is a tribute to all concerned that it is now held in more esteem than ever. Tourists flock from all over the world to walk its acres and stay at the Turnberry Hotel which sits atop a hill, overlooking the course.

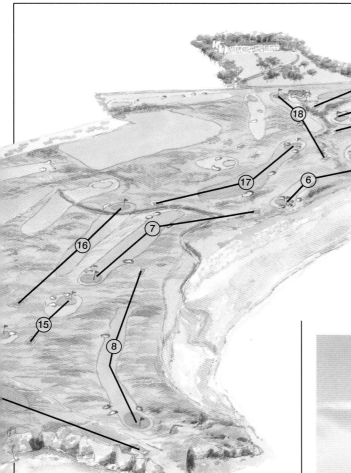

also the scene of the 1961 British Amateur Championship and marked the emergence of Britain's finest post-war amateur golfer. Here Michael Bonallack registered the first of his five victories in the event, and he could hardly have done so in more imperious fashion. The only time he was obliged to play the last two holes was during the morning round of the 36- hole final. It was a performance fully in line with that of Nicklaus and Watson in 1977, and Norman in 1986. Turnberry is that kind of course. It inspires.

A golfer's eye view of the 9th illustrates even more graphically the intimidating nature of this tee shot.

Woe-be-Tide

The seaside holes at Turnberry begin with the alluring par-three 4th which measures 167 yards, and where the line is over the edge of a sandy bay. Not inappropriately, it is called 'Woe-be-Tide'. The 5th is a long par-four, but presents few of the length problems of another short hole, the 6th. This is one of those instances where to refer to a par-three as a short hole is to stretch journalistic license. It measures 222 yards, and is often played into the wind – in which case it may be out of reach of even a driver. The 9th and 10th, though, are probably the two jewels. The first hole of the inward half takes us past the ruins of a castle, the base, it is said, for some of Robert the Bruce's dashing deeds. It is set alongside the rocky shore, and the golfer from the Monterey peninsula might almost feel a sense of *déjà vu* here.

The 15th is another classic short hole, which proved the making of Watson in 1977, when he sank an outrageous 40ft putt from off the green to startle Nicklaus. The 16th, with a burn in front of the green, proved the undoing of Great Britain and Ireland's Walker Cup golfers in 1963. With the wind against, many players underclubbed their approach shots, and the wee burn was full of wee British golf balls. Turnberry was

THE TOURNAMENTS

THE AUSTRALIAN OPEN

With a history dating back to 1904, the Australian Open is one of golf's oldest events, and has survived the passage of time well. Today it is as respected as it has ever been, and although it is held in December, at the end of a tiring season, and involves lengthy journeys, it always attracts a high quality international field. In 1989, the only major championship winner who did not show up was Payne Stewart. It was not always that way, of course, although the lack of rapid transport explains the absence of international support until air travel became commonplace in the 1960s. However the first winner was a foreigner, the Honourable Michael Scott, later a member of Britain's Walker Cup team.

Thereafter the event was dominated, not unnaturally, by players from the host country until the South Africans led overseas interest in the 1950s. In 1955 Bobby Locke prevailed; but the man who really took a shine to the event was Gary Player, who would win it no less than seven times in the years 1958-74. This is just another facet of the remarkable Player story, a man who could truly be called world class since he won wherever golf was played.

The tournament enjoyed some halcyon days at this stage, with Player, the local hero Peter Thomson, Jack Nicklaus and Arnold Palmer, all taking victory bows. Indeed, no other player's name made the trophy other than these four from 1962 to 1972. With six titles to his name, Nicklaus's record in this event is almost as impressive as Player's.

Into the 80s and Americans have as often been on the winning podium as Australians. Tom Watson, Bill Rogers, and Mark Calcavecchia, the three Americans who won the British Open Championship in the 80s, were also, interestingly enough, the three Americans who also won this title during this decade. Inevitably, there were a couple of successes too for Greg Norman, but one of the more impressive wins came in 1989 for an unheralded Aussie, Peter Senior. He defeated a quality field by no less than seven shots after four magnificently consistent rounds that contained 19 birdies, 51 pars, and just two bogeys.

Peter Senior, on his way to an enormously impressive victory in the Australian Open. In a career that has seen more than its fair share of despair, this was a notable and popular triumph.

THE BRITISH AMATEUR CHAMPIONSHIP

It goes almost without saying that the best days of the British Amateur Championship belong to a bygone age, to an era when men did not rush off to the professional ranks at the first whiff of success. Once the British Amateur, like its United States counterpart, was part of the Grand Slam, but now most players treat it as a formal step in their education towards professional graduation. For all that, the Amateur retains a special atmosphere. You can feel on the first day that this is an event which evokes memories with which few professional events can compare. It represents an occasion where you can still enjoy golf without the obstacle of ropes, of massive crowds, and it is played at a pace that does not wither the concentration. It is an event that still matters.

The British Amateur was first played for in 1885. It got off to the weirdest of starts. The instigators were the Royal Liverpool Club at Hoylake who organized a 'tournament open to all amateur golfers.' For that first year, matches that were tied after 18 holes did not go into extra holes but were simply replayed. Byes were not eliminated in the first round, and as there were 48 entries, only three players won through to the semi-finals! A local member, Allan MacFie, was the fortunate man to receive the bye but then he probably needed it. It had taken him 54 holes to get past his fourth round opponent and then it had required the first hole in one in the Amateur (at the 13th) to prevail. Such fortune indicated it was his week and it was. He defeated Horace Hutchinson in the final 7 and 6.

Not surprisingly, some of the rules were changed the following year at St. Andrews. Needless to say, the replayed matches rule was one of those that went by the board. After that the championship settled down nicely. The dominant figure in the early years was Hoylake's John Ball, who went on to win the event on no less than eight occasions in the 24 years from 1888 to 1912. In 1926, a victory for the American Jess Sweetser set a pattern of American victories in a Walker Cup year in Britain. Four years later, it was

The immortal Bobby Jones, the greatest amateur the game has known, pictured with the British Amateur trophy in his golden year of 1930.

the turn of Bobby Jones, the first leg of his immortal Grand Slam.

The Amateur was the only major championship that Jones won only once; how appropriate that it should be at St. Andrews, where the affection ran deep and both ways. In 1933, the Honourable Michael Scott, who had won the Australian Open no less than 29 years earlier, became the oldest recorded winner at 54. A year later and another landmark: Lawson Little of

Newport, Rhode Island, triumphed over Jack Wallace from the West of Scotland by 14 and 13, the biggest-ever victory margin. Little's brilliance was apparent the next year when he successfully defended the title. What made the achievement unique is that

Michael Bonallack won five British Amateur Championships. His presence is still felt as Secretary of the Royal and Ancient.

he won the American Amateur in those two years as well. Fortunately for the non-paid ranks, he turned professional the next year (he won the U.S. Open in 1940).

In 1949, the Championship went for the first and only time to the Republic of Ireland (Portmarnock) and was won by a Northern Irishman, Max Mc-Cready. The bicentennial of the Royal and Ancient in 1954 culminated in a remarkable double for Australia. While Peter Thomson was winning the British Open, his fellow country-man Doug Bachli won the Amateur. For the Victoria Club in Melbourne, the celebrations were everlasting: both Bachli and Thomson were members.

Bonallack's Hat-trick

As the 50s drew to a close so did the influence of the great Irishman Joe Carr reach its pinnacle. He was to win three Amateurs in all, a feat that had not been performed by a British or Irish golfer for over half a century. Then, as Carr's era passed into history, Michael Bonallack's began. He was to win no less than five Amateur Championships including one over Carr in 1968. That win signalled the first of three in a row for Bonallack which remains a record. These days Bonallack still attends every Amateur and indeed every British Open – in his capacity as Secretary of the Royal & Ancient Golf Club of St. Andrews.

No-one has since dominated amateur golf like Bonallack did and no-one will. Peter McEvoy won the event twice and was a beaten finalist once, and defeated Bonallack's England records, without ever displaying the same omnipotence. These days no-one with any raw talent stays an amateur after the age of 24. So in one respect McEvoy has had the last word. We can safely say he is the last of a dying breed, the last of the great British amateurs.

THE BRITISH OPEN CHAMPIONSHIP

The British Open, first played in 1860, is the grandfather of the four major championships. Today this prestigious tournament welcomes players from every country wherever the Royal and Ancient game is played and enjoys the most widely international field of all the majors.

It is ironic, then, that the very first Open was not an open event at all but a 'closed' one. Only professionals were allowed to enter, and only eight bothered. Three circuits of Prestwick's 12-hole layout were played and Willie Park won by two strokes from 'Old Tom' Morris. He received a red leather belt, resembling the Lonsdale version awarded to British boxing champions, and like the pugilists, anyone who won it three times in a row was allowed to keep it. This 'Young Tom' Morris did in 1868-70 and in doing so he almost killed off the Open; it was not played the following year.

Upon its resumption in 1872 the belt had been replaced by the silver claret jug that is still played for today. The idea to revive the event had come from the Royal and Ancient Club at St. Andrews, the Honourable Company of Edinburgh golfers at Musselburgh (they later moved to their present home, Muirfield) and Prestwick Golf Club, where the Open had been played every year to that point. Only St. Andrews of the three still stands on the Championship roster but for the next 24 years, these three courses hosted the event in turns.

The Great Triumvirate

By the close of the century, golf was dominated by the 'Great Triumvirate' of Harry Vardon, J. H. Taylor and James Braid. They brought to the game a professionalism that foreshadowed the modern era. Vardon, indeed, won the event six times, which remains a record. By this time, the tournament was growing in stature with Royal St. George's, Sandwich, becoming the first English course on the championship roster.

Over the years, 14 venues have had the honor of staging an Open, but these days the active number is down

Willie Park (left), the first winner of the British Open, and Harry Vardon (below) who triumphed on a record six occasions. Vardon was part of the Great Trimvirate, bringing to the game a professionalism that pointed the way towards the modern era.

Three of the great names of British Open lore. Bobby Jones (above) shows the style that won him three titles. Jack Nicklaus and Tom Watson (left) during their classic duel in 1977. Watson (right) stands alone in the modern era.

to seven, as the accessories that go alongside the championship, such as the tented village, have ruled out those with little land. The ever-increasing crowds, too, means that this number is likely to diminish rather than increase, a fact the R&A readily admit they would like to change. Golf's governing body took full control of the event after World War I, when the total prize money was $1,000 (£225). For the Muirfield Open in 1991, the likelihood is we shall see the first $2 million (£1 million) British Open.

In 1921, the Open went to the United States for the first time, as the expatriate Scot Jock Hutchison collected the trophy. It was a journey with which the auld claret jug was to become only too familiar. Walter Hagen's arrival on the scene stimulated great transatlantic interest in the event and Americans would dominate the Open between the wars. No-one in Britain minded, for the result was some vintage years for the Open with Hagen himself, Bobby Jones and Gene Sarazen all in their prime. Jones won it in 1926, 1927 and 1930, Hagen twice in 1922 and 1924,

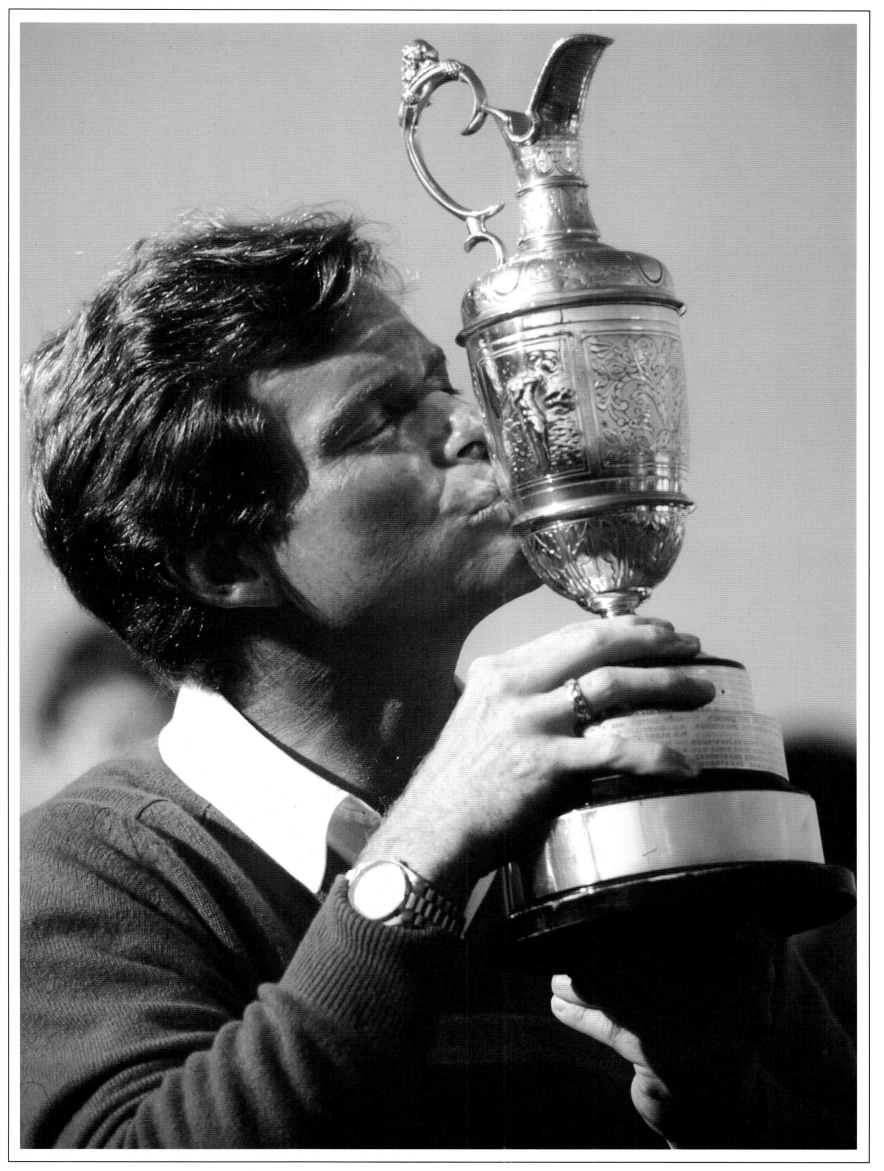

and Sarazen in 1932. For a 13-year period only Arthur Havers, in 1923, prevented the trophy from going to America.

Perhaps bored with their dominance of the event, or by the time it took to reach the British Isles by ship, the top Americans gave up on the Open after Sarazen's victory. The generation that followed preferred to stay at home, and the British Open's prestige suffered as a result of this. It lost its place as the most important championship with greater attention focused on the U.S. Open and the emergence of the Masters. There were three appearances by Sam Snead (one victory in 1946) and one hugely successful visit by Ben Hogan in 1953.

Sixties Revival

If the British Open was ever to recover its eminence it was clear that it needed the arrival on the scene of a modern-day Walter Hagen, an American with a wider perspective on matters. That man arrived in the guise of Arnold Palmer. For in addition to being the father of modern American professional golf, Palmer could also be given patriarchal clothing for the way he revived the Open. After the post-war years had been dominated by the South African Bobby Locke and the Australian Peter Thomson, along came the dashing Palmer at the start of the 60s and it is true to say

that golf was never the same again.

Right behind him was Jack Nicklaus and together with the little South African Gary Player they did much the same for the game as the original Great Triumvirate all those years earlier. They did not have things all their own way. In 1963 the New Zealander Bob Charles became the first and to date only left-hander to win a major championship. And the 1964 St. Andrews Open went to 'champagne' Tony Lema whose life was so tragically terminated later in a plane crash. But the big three breathed life into the event and resuscitated it to such an extent that in 1967 an American television company was prepared to buy the rights to beam the championship back to the States. These days the pictures are beamed by satellite to all points of the compass.

The Watson Era

Since the 60s, the Open has gone from strength to strength. Palmer's contribution has never been forgotten by the R&A who appeared to change the rules of entry so that he retained his exempt status. And quite right too. For there is hardly anything in golf to match the ovation Palmer and, indeed, Nicklaus receive when they walk down the 18th fairway in the Open, irrespective of how they are faring. British golf audiences have never been parochial in this respect. Even in these days when the Brits have their own heroes to cheer,

some of the biggest roars are are still reserved for Arnie, the Golden Bear, and Seve Ballesteros. And a man from Kansas City called Tom Watson. The record books credit Vardon with more Open wins than he, but only the most statistically burdened of souls would dispute that Watson has the finest Open record of anyone. For he achieved his five victories during a golden age for the sport, when competition was at its height, and some of the game's most heroic figures were in their prime.

Watson so loves the Open and the links courses it has always been played on, that he goes over early every year to test his wits on the best of the British seaside courses. If you are playing one such course in the week before the Open, keep an eye out for a still fresh-faced man in a check cap; for one thing you can be sure of is that Watson will seek no special privileges and will just turn up for a game like any other citizen.

European Renaissance

Since the Watson era, the Open has signaled the renaissance of British and European golf, with five victories in the seven events since 1983. Most memorable were two wins by Severiano Ballesteros. In 1984 at St. Andrews, Ballesteros's exuberant victory salute (he had also won at Lytham in 1979) was delivered with all the panache that characterizes his play. And at Lytham in 1988, he closed with a round of 65 which equaled the Open record for a final 18 holes to win the event. The home audience did not mind two of those slotted in between either! Sandy Lyle's triumph in 1985 was the first British win since Tony Jacklin's in 1969. And with Nick Faldo's win two years later, British golf found itself witnessing a halcyon age never before known in the modern era.

It was appropriate though that the decade should end with an American, Mark Calcavecchia, winning. For it meant that in the past seven years, two British players (three wins), one Australian, an American and a Spaniard (twice) had won the event. There we see the championship's cosmopolitan appeal, its broad rallying call to golfers from across the world. That is why its winner deserves the R&A's sub-title, 'the Champion Golfer,' that goes with it.

Sandy Lyle's victory at Royal St George's in 1985 ended 16 lean years for the British game in its 'home' major championship.

THE BRITISH PGA CHAMPIONSHIP

How can a tournament have two champions in any one given year? In 1967 and 1968, the British PGA Championship managed it. Hitherto, it had been a 'closed' event, restricted to professionals from the United Kingdom and Ireland. In 1967, to take into account the growing influx of players from Europe and around the world, the field was widened and so there was a PGA 'Open' Championship and a PGA 'Closed' one. Fortunately, this situation only lasted two years. The PGA, which these days looks after the welfare of the club professionals, began its own championship for their benefit in 1973.

In the early years of the tournament, there were victories for some familiar names from British golf in the 50s and 60s. People like Dai Rees, Harry Bradshaw, Guy Wolstenholme, and Peter Alliss. Perhaps to compensate for the fact there had been two PGAs for two years, there was none at all in 1970 and 1971. After the hiatus, early wins for Tony Jacklin, Peter Oosterhuis and Arnold Palmer re-established its reputation, and, as the decade closed, a young Nick Faldo hinted at the imperious form he would strike in the late 80s by winning the event three times in four years.

In 1982, there was a stirring second triumph for Jacklin at Hillside. Jacklin's career at the time was thought to be long over. He cut a sad figure, tormented by the part of his game, putting, where he had once proved so inspirational. Still the galleries flocked to watch him for his deeds of yore: after all, if you've got it, charisma stays long after the putting has gone. His followers longed for the return of the 'real' Jacklin and at Hillside there was the last authentic glimpse. He was helped by an awful attack of the putting 'yips' by Bernhard Langer on the next to last hole. The popular West German has experienced contrasting fortunes in this event. In 1987, those putting problems were long forgotten as he won the tournament by a mile. He went round Wentworth's West Course in a scarcely credible four-round total of 270, 18 under par. In the previous two years, the winning scores had been 281 and 282. No wonder the runner-up Severiano Ballesteros said sportingly: 'Bernhard

Dai Rees was one of the best-loved of British professionals and it was his victories in the British PGA Championship during the 50s that helped establish his popularity.

played the game as well as it can be played today.'

But a year later, it was all change once more, as the 'yips' returned to haunt the defending champion. He had led at the halfway stage but seizure set in on virtually every green thereafter and he finished the tournament a sad figure. Another year-long battle to control this cruellest of golfing afflictions was about to begin.

The tournament had moved to Wentworth, the home of the PGA European Tour, in 1984, and it is now staged there every year. Since its return — it was played there for three successive years in the 70s — the tour has steadily upgraded it to the extent where attendance by the top European players is all but mandatory, even if appearance money in one form or another is paid as a sweetener. It is now the tour's flagship event, which is as it should be, of course, with such a name as the PGA Championship.

Fighting Finishes

In recent years, in addition to Langer's memorable golf, there have been some excellent finishes. Looking back to 1985 provides a poignant reminder of just how good the now struggling Paul Way was. That year, he tied on a 72-hole total of 282 with Sandy Lyle, who has never won this event. On the second extra hole, it was the precocious Way who broke the deadlock, finding the green of this massive par five with a drive and a fearless 3-wood. Substantial compensation for Lyle, of course, came in the form of the British Open two months later.

In 1989, Ian Woosnam, who played amateur golf with Lyle, won while playing what he considered to be mediocre golf. The runner-up, Zimbabwean Mark McNulty, perhaps gave a more accurate summary of Woosnam's 14-under par winning score. 'You don't have to listen to this bull,' he said. 'Ian is hitting the ball just perfectly.'

Ian Woosnam's success at Wentworth in 1989 continued the thread of Welsh victories began by Dai Rees two decades earlier. Here he shows the power that makes him such an exciting talent.

THE COLONIAL NATIONAL INVITATION

The staggering growth in prize money through the 1980s forced some of the older events on the U.S. and other tours, to rethink their views about corporate sponsorship. 'I hope we never have to become something like the Coca-Cola Masters,' Hord Hardin, Tournament chairman at Augusta, said a few years ago, echoing the views of many directors of long-established events. But whereas the Masters, because it is a major championship, will always draw the top players whether it offers $3 million in prize money or $3, other tournaments know they either follow the spiralling prize money trend or be consigned to backwater status. So it is that events like the Colonial National Invitation consider it better to be known as the Southwestern Bell Colonial rather than not be known at all. After 42 years getting by without it, they finally gave in to reality in 1988 and let big business pick up the tab.

Whatever its name, it is one of the great events on the tour, played on a magnificent golf course, with a history dating back to 1946. The local boy Ben Hogan won it four years out of the first six, and the event has been associated with his name ever since. The Colonial is both a golf course and a tournament. They were the creations of Texas businessman Marvin Leonard, who detested the Bermuda grass found on most Texas greens because its coarseness distorts the science of putting.

His logical suggestion that the greens at his local club be converted to bent grass was rejected. Bent grass would not thrive in the hot Texas sun, he was told. The answer so frustrated him he decided to build his own course at Fort Worth and see for himself. The result was Colonial, a masterpiece – with superlative bent-grass greens.

Given such a course – it is over 7,150 yards long and one of the most difficult in North America – it is no surprise to see some familiar names gracing the Marvin Leonard Trophy that goes to the winner. Like the Masters, this annual event is one of the landmarks of Spring, and also like the Masters, as its name implies, it is an invitation event.

This can lead to passes for overseas players for whom the exempt tour means they cannot otherwise get to play. In 1989, it led to a victory for one such competitor, the Australian, Ian Baker-Finch.

The iceman Ben Hogan (top) has been a permanent fixture at the Colonial since winning the inaugural tournament in 1946. The local boy has seen it grow and achieve eminence on the international stage, thanks to victories such as that by the Australian Ian Baker-Finch (above).

THE CURTIS CUP

The weather might have necessitated gloves but the news of rare British successes kept the home captain Diane Bailey warm in 1988.

In many respects the Curtis Cup has followed the path of the men's equivalent, the Walker Cup, with overwhelming American superiority being seriously challenged only in recent years. And like the Walker Cup, the impetus for the contest also came from the United States. In this instance, the inspiration was two sisters, Harriet and Margaret Curtis of Boston, who had played in an international match at Cromer in England, as early as 1905.

It was not until 1932, however, that a cup bearing their name was played for in the biennial form which we recognize today. For the leading women amateurs of the United States and Great Britain and Ireland it remains the premier team competition. Mind you, calling it a competition would until recently have been to stretch credibility: for most of those contests American superiority was absolute.

The 36-hole format was hardly an aid to close matches, serving merely to reflect the dominance of the Americans. Although they halved the 1936 match, Great Britain and Ireland had to wait another 16 years for a first success, and then followed it with a second victory in the next home match at Prince's, Sandwich, in 1956.

The 1950s was a strong decade for British women's golf and in 1958, the team successfully defended the trophy with the second halved match of the series to date, and the first in America. Remarkably the outcome of this Curtis Cup rested with the same two women as in the previous contest. At Prince's, Frances ('Bunty') Smith had prevailed on the 36th hole against Polly Riley to win her match and therefore the cup for Britain. Two years later, and once more the tie between these two went to the last. Once more Mrs Smith won, this time to secure the overall half.

American Dominance

Hopes were high that this sequence of British success would continue into the next decade. In 1960, the venue was Lindrick, the scene of a rare Great Britain and Ireland Ryder Cup victory three years earlier. There was to be no repeat. Mrs Smith's remarkable Curtis Cup career ended after the foursomes. She did not play in the singles and so ended with an unbeaten record stretching over five matches.

It was the signal for the Americans to acquire the aura of omnipotence once more. Starting at Lindrick they would win no less than 13 straight matches stretching over 26 years. In 1962, the British team showed five new names, but suffered its worst defeat to date, by the margin of 8-1. Two years later the format was changed to 18-hole matches and it produced a fine contest at

Royal Porthcawl in Wales. The teams were level with three singles matches remaining on the course. But a win for Peggy Conley, at 17 the youngest-ever Curtis Cup competitor at the time, over Bridget Jackson, was the moment for the Americans to assume control. They won the last two matches as well to run out three-point winners.

The match now settled into a pattern. The games in Britain would be relatively close affairs, with the conditions and terrain acting rather like a handicap system. Conversely, when the familiarity was with the Americans, the final result was usually a hefty U.S. victory.

Britain Fights Back

Towards the end of the 80s, the fate of both the Ryder and the Curtis Cups followed a remarkably similar pattern. The respective British captains, Tony Jacklin and Diane Bailey, shared a common belief that while it did mean a great deal to take part in such matches, it would actually be rather nice to win once in a while as well. In their first outings as captains both lost by just one point, but after Jacklin had inspired a Belfry victory in 1985, Bailey led her troops to the most remarkable of wins in Kansas in 1986.

It was the first time a British team had ever won on American soil, which was an historic achievement in itself, but what was perhaps even more astonishing was the size of the victory margin. A win by 13-5 equalled the largest since the event reverted to 18-hole matches

The Curtis Cup is virtually American property. In 1984 the captain, Phyllis Preuss (top) held the trophy aloft, signaling the 13th consecutive triumph by the US. In 1990 (above), the faces were different but the studious approach, and the result, was the same.

and is far and away the largest ever managed by any visiting side.

Just for good measure, and just as Jacklin's team did, they successfully defended the trophy two years later at Royal St George's. In the first 54 years of the competition Great Britain and Ireland had won just twice. Now they had won two out of two, and British women's amateur golf had acquired new levels of respect. But American pride was hurt and in 1990 they exact-

ed a heavy retribution. At the Somerset Hills course, New Jersey, the host nation won back the trophy by the crushing margin of 14-4.

THE DUNHILL CUP

Never one to miss a commercial opportunity, Mark McCormack noted the decline of the World Cup and launched his own Dunhill Nations Cup in 1985. 'It is the most significant new golf competition for many years,' he announced. The prize fund was set at $1.2 million – twice that of the richest European stroke-play event, the British Open Championship. In order to confer some traditional dignity on the event, it was held at St. Andrews; and while at the time there were mutterings about taking it to other countries, there it has remained ever since.

The Dunhill has a unique format. Each country has three representatives, who compete on a medal-matchplay basis: that is, they play 18 holes strokeplay against a member of the opposition and the one who takes the fewer shots is the winner. The format has many critics but it is fair to say it has stimulated some moments of high drama and enhanced St. Andrews' long history on at least one occasion. That was when Curtis Strange set the Old Course record of 62 strokes.

The great Road Hole, the 17th, ensures that no player can relax, even if he is three shots ahead at that point. (Of course, if he had such a lead in straight matchplay, he and his opponent would be walking back to the clubhouse.)

The pick of the Dunhill Cups held to date was Ireland's memorable triumph in 1988. In the final against Australia, the match between Rodger Davis and Des Smyth illustrated what can happen under the medal-matchplay format. The Australian Davis was one ahead going to the 17th, but there, sliced his drive out of bounds and ran up a seven. Smyth took four and from being one down – and his country out of the event he was two up and Ireland on the brink of an historic triumph.

Despite that reverse, the Australians have won the competition twice, England once, while the United States finally got their name on the trophy in 1989. This event was held the week after the momentous tied Ryder Cup match at The Belfry, and in the 36-hole final against Japan, Mark Calcavecchia helped overcome the inevitable sense of anti-climax by going round the Old Course in 67 shots in the morning and 66 in the afternoon.

The Dunhill Cup became America's cup for the first time in 1989. Their team, Curtis Strange, Tom Kite, and Mark Calcavecchia find the ideal backdrop to show off the trophy whilst basking in some golden October sunshine.

THE DUNLOP PHOENIX

Towards the end of November, the Japanese circuit runs a three-week international tour when the fields are traditionally peppered with overseas players. The sequence begins with the Visa Taiheiyo Masters, ends with the Casio World Open, and sandwiched in between is the biggest of the three, the Dunlop Phoenix. Alongside the Australian Open, this is the premier event during what are the winter months in the Northern Hemisphere. 'Everything is just perfect,' says the 1990 Masters champion Nick Faldo. 'The course, the tournament, the hotel and the location are all as good as we find all year.' The Phoenix field is never less than first-class, and many of the international players are happy to fall into line with local customs for the week.

A regular attender is Tom Watson, who has employed the same 4ft 9in Japanese woman caddie every year. They make a great pair. The woman in question, Masayo Fuse, insists on making a big fuss over the five-times British Open champion, as she fills in the divots, cleans the clubs, and tows a golf bag as big as she is around Phoenix Country Club in southern Japan. Masayo Fuse is not alone. The Japanese caddies generally form quite an attachment to the international players and often knit headcovers and the like to mark their annual visit to Japan.

The strength of the American contingent in particular is reflected in the fact that U.S. players have won the title in nine of the last 12 years. In 1988, only one Japanese player, Hajime Meshiai, made the top 10, but a year later, two of the three fabled Ozaki brothers, Naomichi and Tateo, or Jet and Joe, as the outside world knows them, penetrated the top four.

One man for whom this three-week leg has proved beneficial is the former Masters champion, Larry Mize who in 1989 added the Phoenix title to the World Open he had won the year before. His first prize was 29 million yen ($200,000)!

Tom Watson (pictured here during the 1989 Ryder Cup) is a huge name in Japan and a regular attender of their premier tournaments, prominent amongst which is the Dunlop Phoenix.

THE EUROPEAN OPEN

With a tented village that seems to covers half of south-east England for the tournament's duration, it is clear that the European Open is an event that has caught the public imagination. Those from beyond Europe appear to like it as well if the cast list of trophy winners is anything to go by: two Americans, an Australian, and a Japanese were among the first six winners.

Isao Aoki had shown his liking for London's suburban 'stockbroker belt' when he won the 1978 World Matchplay Championship at Wentworth. Now, here he was, just a few miles away at Sunningdale, adding one of

No success was more widely welcomed in 1989 than that of Andrew Murray in the European Open. It was some compensation for a career blighted by an arthritic condition, spondylitis.

Europe's top strokeplay titles to his collection. In the aforementioned hospitality tents, champagne glasses were being charged in no uncertain terms. For the year of Aoki's victory, 1983, was the year that the Japanese electronics firm, Panasonic, took over as corporate sponsor.

The European Open began in 1978 at Walton Heath, Surrey, before Sandy Lyle won an event at Turnberry that was almost blown away by gales. A return to Walton Heath was followed by a visit to Royal Liverpool and then Sunningdale became the event's home for five years. Perhaps the most memorable occasion was Greg Norman's triumph in his all-conquering year of 1986. He said he could break 60 round the Old Course, and the way he was playing that year, few openly disagreed. Well, that mark in the end eluded him, but ample financial compensation came in the form of a

$160,000 bonus for collecting the British Open Championship and European Open titles in the same year.

With the Walker Cup to be staged at Sunningdale in 1987, the European Open moved back to Walton Heath, and now the event alternates between there and Sunningdale, thus enjoying the splendor of two of the finest inland golf courses in Britain.

The return to Walton Heath has seen two of the most poignant victories. In 1987, Paul Way, who had looked the most precocious of players in winning the British PGA Championship and playing in the 1985 Ryder Cup, but who had since drifted aimlessly, suddenly found his best form to register an unlikely triumph. And then Andrew Murray came along in 1989. The victory cheque of $100,000 was more than Murray had earned in the whole of his previous 10 years on the European tour!

THE EUROPEAN MASTERS

This event started life as the Swiss Open, but a change in name in 1983 to the European Masters reflects the way it has been upgraded to its current status as one of Europe's top-drawer events. The prize money is regularly the highest for a strokeplay event on the European Tour, and over the years quite a few of the top Americans have been lured to play.

One incentive to make the trip is the breathtaking Alpine scenery the perennial venue, Crans-sur-Sierre, affords. The sloping fairways that make for a sea of green during the tournament are an ocean of pure white in the winter and double up as ski slopes. Its high altitude means the ball travels 10 percent further than at sea level, and while the stupendous views can be distracting, the course is full of par-fours that can be reached in one and par-fives in two. Indeed, many of the European Tour's low-scoring records, have been set at Crans. In 1971, the Italian Baldovino Dassu went around in just 60, a score which included 11 birdies. Both are records, as is the nine-under 27 that Spaniard José-Maria Canizares recorded for the first nine holes in 1978. There are some who feel that the 'pitch and putt' nature of Crans is not in keeping with the event's prize fund and status; but the names on the trophy show the tournament has generally produced a quality champion, albeit with the odd surprise winner fitted in.

The Swiss Open had a long and proud history stretching back to 1923. The first winner was Alec Ross, who claimed the title in three of its first four years. The move to Crans was made in 1939, although only one Swiss Open was held there before World War II and its aftermath caused an eight-year break in the event.

The only player to have won the event three times at Crans is Severiano Ballesteros who claimed back-to-back titles in 1977 and 1978, before winning again in 1989, by two shots over the Australian Craig Parry.

No-one enjoys the clean Swiss air of Crans more than Spain's José-Maria Canizares. In 1978 he played the front nine in 27 and 12 years on, while finishing second, was still talking about going round in the near mythical score of 59.

THE LANCÔME TROPHY

Mark McCormack is as controversial a figure in golf as he is in tennis, but it would be churlish to deny his substantial contribution to the health of European golf in the autumn months. Three of the most eagerly-anticipated events take place in September and October, and all were his ideas. The first was the World Matchplay Championship, the most recent the Dunhill Cup and sandwiched in between was the Lancôme Trophy. Along with the French amateur golfer Gatean Mourgue d'Algue, he conceived the event to be a European 'Champion of Champions' tournament and while the field these days numbers around 70 and

so stretches McCormack's ideal, that is broadly the strength of it.

The venue, St-Nom-La-Bretèche, which is on the outskirts of Versailles, has held every event since its inception in 1970. In truth it is a somewhat ordinary course, although Severiano Ballesteros rates it among his favorites. This may have something to do with the fact that it is one of his favored hunting grounds. In all, he has been successful on four occasions, including a highly unusual, if not unique, 'share' of the trophy in 1986. That year, he and the West German Bernhard Langer made all the running and after 72 holes they could not be

separated. After the sudden death play-off had gone on for four holes, they were still tied and now darkness had all but fallen. Both men had commitments the following day, so Tour officials declared the result a tie, with both players sharing the title for six months each.

Over the years the Lancôme Trophy has gathered a truly cosmopolitan list of winners. Four of the first five victors were Americans, including Johnny Miller and Arnold Palmer, but since then, the highly unusual (some would argue typically French!) trophy of a man's torso with a golf ball embedded in his right breast, has been won by Australians and South Africans in addition to Europeans and Americans. And in 1989, it went to Argentina, as the 35-year-old Eduardo Romero from Córdoba put together an impressive finish to deny José-Maria Olazábal.

Seve Ballesteros rates the Lancôme course one of his favorites. Having won the trophy four times he is a primary reason why golf is undergoing an unprecedented surge of popularity in France.

THE MEMORIAL

The three greatest American golfers of the post-war era all have an event on the U.S. Tour associated with their name. Ben Hogan started the ball rolling with the Colonial. Arnold Palmer's is the Nestlé Invitational at Bay Hill. And the newest was instigated by Jack Nicklaus and is known as The Memorial. All three are on courses that the players built themselves. The Memorial may be the newest, but is perhaps the most prestigious of the trio, and is played every year on Jack's masterpiece, Muirfield Village, near his home town of Columbus, Ohio.

The venue and the style of the tournament very much reflect the lasting impression made upon Nicklaus by Bobby Jones's work at Augusta with the Masters tournament. The rather odd choice of title is partly explained by the fact that, each year, the tournament honors one of the great names in golf. The choice each season is decided by a Captains Club, made up of 15 people who have given lasting service to the game, such as past presidents of the United States Golf Association. The problem is that some of the names they have come up with are still in the land of the living, which rather defeats the Memorial bit. It was a discrepancy recognized by Hogan, who when his name was put forward to join the list, said rather abruptly: 'They can choose me when I am dead.' For all that, no-one would grumble with those selected to date. The first, not surprisingly was Jones. In 1989, it was the three times British Open champion, Sir Henry Cotton.

Unusually for Nicklaus, this was one of the few event conceived during his professional career which he did not win in the inaugural year. That honour went to Roger Maltbie. Nicklaus had to wait until year two. 'This is probably the hardest tournament for me to win of any I have ever won,' he said at the prize ceremony. It probably explains why he has won it only twice, the other occasion being in 1984.

Jack Nicklaus is the greatest name the game has known and the Memorial Tournament in his hometown, on the course he built, is his legacy to the US tour he helped to establish.

Bean Baits 'The Bear'

That was one of the most memorable of the Memorials played to date. With 14 holes to play, Nicklaus seemed to have the title all wrapped up, when Andy Bean put together a startling sequence of scores on such a tough course. He registered seven birdies in the next nine holes to tie Nicklaus at nine under and so set the scene for a grandstand finish. On the 17th, with Bean safely down the middle, Nicklaus carved his drive way right and out of bounds. It needed the inner strength which has always been his greatest virtue to hit a 4-iron second shot to 25ft and hole the putt for a bogey to trail by only one.

On the last, Nicklaus again drove into trouble leaving him no shot to the green. Bean was safely on the back in two, and when Nicklaus chipped to 4ft, and Bean 3ft, we had a classic match-play situation. If Nicklaus missed it was all over; but if he holed, it would leave Bean with a short putt that would fully test his nerve. Nicklaus did hole, Bean, alas, did not. No-one can let Nicklaus off like that and expect to get away with it. The Golden Bear triumphed on the third extra hole.

Over the years the tournament, which is always played in mid-May, has been plagued by bad weather. Indeed on several occasions, such has been the rain that officials have had to resort to using 'winter rules.' Such was the case in 1989. But the year before the course played true and fast and the winner was Curtis Strange, who went

Andy Bean resembles Jack Nicklaus in build and demeanour on the course and in the 1984 Memorial he matched him shot for shot as well.

from there to collect his first major championship win, the Open, just a couple of weeks later. Strange dazzled over the last two days, returning scores of 64 and 67 to win from Hale Irwin, who like Nicklaus has won the event twice, and the South African David Frost.

Despite its youth, The Memorial is a tour event with few peers. One day, and it is to be hoped it is a long way in the future, it is likely to prove a truly fitting memorial to the most successful golfer who ever lived.

THE RYDER CUP

Of all the extraordinary events that happened in golf in the 1980s, none told so remarkable a tale as the Ryder Cup. For the match that began the decade as a backwater event of minimal interest to the American players, public and media, ended with one magazine declaring World War III as its contribution to winning the cup back. *Golf Digest* caricatured Raymond Floyd as the legendary General Patton in a ludicrous exercise in hype. Thankfully, Floyd, one of the sport's fiercest competitors, was blessed with a rather more sensible approach. 'The most important thing is that golf wins,' Floyd said. 'The most important triumph will be one for integrity.' Thus, in 1989, did the American captain preserve the spirit of the event in an age vastly different to that in which it had begun.

The man who donated the trophy, Samuel Ryder, was hardly a golfer at all. Indeed, if he had not moved his business as a seed merchant to the south of England, the contest might never have got started. There, late in life, he took up golf under the tutelage of Abe Mitchell, and (whether at Mitchell's suggestion or not is unclear) he presented a cup for competition between the professionals of America and Great Britain and Ireland.

Inaugural Match

The first match was played in 1927 at the Worcester club in Massachusetts. The British team, captained by the veteran Ted Ray, were no match for their counterparts led by the legendary Walter Hagen, and were on the receiving end of a 9-2 thrashing, illustrating just how far American golf had come in such a short space of time. However, during the early years, American superiority did not always show itself. The

British proved more than a match on their own territory. Two years later, they exacted immediate compensation by winning at Moortown, and won again the next time the match was played in Britain, at Southport & Ainsdale in 1933. This was the best match yet, with the outcome resting on the last match on the course. The home team scraped through when the American Densmore Shute, that year's British Open champion, three-putted the final green.

Post-War Years

And that was it, so far as British success was concerned, for 24 years. After World War II, the British team travelled to Oregon, financed by a local American businessman. Charity remained at his home. On the course, the

Vastly different generations, reflected by the style of dress. But the intense level of concentration was the same whether it was Leo Diegel in 1929 (above) or Ian Woosnam and Nick Faldo (left) 58 years later. Everyone gives it their best shot when it comes to the Ryder Cup.

Americans marched to their biggest triumph yet, by a margin of 11-1. The War had significantly widened the difference in class between the two teams. In the years following 1945, America experienced an economic boom, and the professional golf circuit was among the beneficiaries. In Britain, the picture could hardly have been more different, with rationing still in existence, and people struggling to pick up the pieces of their fragmented lives.

And so it was 1953 before the first top-class match took place after the war. This time the venue was Wentworth, when Britain reached the brink of victory, only to falter in the inexper-

Undoubtedly Sam Torrance's finest moment and one of Europe's too. The Scot can hardly believe it as he sinks the winning putt in 1985.

disastrous with the home team winning by the biggest margin yet, $23\frac{1}{2}$-$8\frac{1}{2}$. It was not until 1969, that a match, in the true sense of the word, took place in this decade and then it was the most memorable to date.

England Expects

That year Tony Jacklin had whetted home expectations with his British Open victory and the crowds flocked to Royal Birkdale. They were not disappointed. What followed over three memorable days fully illustrated the exciting vagaries of matchplay golf. The last day began with the sides locked in a tie, and it ended that way. Jacklin had defeated Jack Nicklaus in the morning singles matches and took him on once more in the afternoon. This time it was a far closer affair. When Jacklin holed a huge putt on the 17th it meant they went to the last all-square. Excitement consumed Southport and an enormous roar had gone up when Jacklin holed that putt. Up ahead, Brian Huggett holed a five-footer for a courageous half against Billy Casper and by doing so thought he had won the Ryder Cup.

He had been deceived by the crowd following Jacklin's game into believing the British Open champion had won. Now the outcome rested on the final hole of the final game. After three shots, Jacklin lay three feet away, Nicklaus four. The Golden Bear holed, and then conceded Jacklin's putt in one of the great sporting gestures. 'I don't think you would have missed and in any case I am not going to give you the chance,' Nicklaus told Jacklin.

After the excitement of Birkdale it was back to American domination. So complete was it that after the 1977 match at Lytham, Nicklaus wrote to Lord Derby, President of the British PGA, saying he feared the match might die unless the format was changed. He suggested the British side be augmented with the best players from the rapidly developing European scene. The Ryder Cup committee decided to vary the Deed of Trust under the powers vested in them, and acted in the way Nicklaus suggested.

European Intervention

No change was immediately apparent. The Europeans shot themselves in the

ienced hands of Peter Alliss and Bernard Hunt, who both missed short putts on the final green. Had they holed them, Britain would have won instead of losing, $7\frac{1}{2}$-$4\frac{1}{2}$. Four years later, and wiser, the pair were back when the home team did finally triumph, at Lindrick. American strength, however, remained the dominant factor in the overall scheme of things.

In 1963, fourball matches were introduced to try and fuel some American interest but all that did was emphasize their superiority. Britain managed just one fourball victory out of eight. The next match in America was even more foot in 1981 by omitting Severiano Ballesteros after a series of acrimonious rows. The Americans won easily. But now two changes brought about a remarkable upsurge in Ryder Cup fortunes. The first was the appointment of Jacklin as Ryder Cup captain. He insisted that it would be 'first class all the way' for the next match in America. He argued that if you seat people in the rear of an aircraft and in the cheapest of hotels, they will live down to your expectations. The second change was to involve Ballesteros up to his neck in the Ryder Cup. Jacklin told him that he was the best player in the world and pivotal to any European hope of success. Ballesteros did not much care

for the Americans anyway, who he felt had treated him shabbily when he first went there.

It did not happen in 1983 in Florida but the Americans had been duly warned. The margin between the sides was a single point, the visitors' best performance yet in America. Two years later came an historic European victory, the first time the Americans had lost for 18 years. The Belfry was the scene of delirious celebrations, with Concorde dipping its wings overhead, and the crowd sprayed with champagne by the players perched on the Belfry rooftops.

Two years later, even those scenes were bettered, when the Europeans

claimed that cherished first-ever win on U.S. soil. Moreover they did so in Nicklaus's backyard at Muirfield Village, and over a side he captained. Nicklaus recognized the irony of it all. Interest in the match had certainly been revived with the inclusion of the Europeans!

Floyd's Fightback

And so to 1989 and a match so feverishly anticipated by the British audience

The stars and stripes were out in force at The Belfry in 1989 as the wives added their support to the US bid to recapture the trophy.

A view from the back of a packed grandstand as European captain Tony Jacklin runs on to the home green to congratulate Jose-Maria Canizares. But the USA won the last four singles to secure an honorable half.

that it became the first all-ticket golf tournament in European history. The scene was once more The Belfry, a course that had opened just 13 years earlier. Ironically, Floyd had been present at that inaugural ceremony, flown in to hit the first ball on the Brabazon

course as the reigning Masters champion.

Now he was back as Ryder Cup captain, having spent a season preparing with a thoroughness the like of which no American skipper had shown before. Of course, there had hardly been any need before. But now the American press had gathered in force, the players were primed, and interest in the match in America and Europe scaled new heights.

It proved a case of the immovable force meeting the irresistible object.

The match was perhaps the most memorable of all, and played against a backdrop of consummate sportsmanship. 'The Greatest Sporting Show on Earth' was how one newspaper headlined it, and no-one felt inclined to disagree. Both sides had their chances to win on the most absorbing of final days, and in the end one of the great Ryder Cup shots from Curtis Strange ensured the contest ended in only the second tie. As it turned out, not only had golf 'won,' as Floyd had hoped, it was the only winner.

THE TOURNAMENT PLAYERS' CHAMPIONSHIP

The Tournament Players' Championship was inaugurated in the same year (1974) that Deane Beman became the United States Tour commissioner, and since then he has tried everything in his power to get the tournament accepted as the fifth major championship.

The majors don't have a pro-am? Ok, we'll cancel the pro-am. The majors don't have a corporate sponsor? Neither will we. In 1988, the title was changed to The Players' Championship because it seems to suggest the one thing the event does not have: tradition. Beman was not amused when

Sandy Lyle won in 1987. Normally the winner mouths a few anodyne phrases like 'yes, I think this is the fifth major – it always attracts the best players,' guaranteed to make the tournament committee smile complacently. Sandy, asked what the difference was between winning the British Open at Sandwich, and this tournament, replied: 'Oh, about 100 years.'

No man, not even Beman, can set out to create a major. What Lyle was alluding to was the fact that they evolve over time, and such is the public acceptance of the four in place it seems unlikely that that number will ever change.

What we can say for Beman and The Players' Championship is that it is probably the fifth most desirable tournament to win, but still a good way behind the first four. It is held every year on the TPC's own course at their headquarters in Sawgrass, Florida. It is an annual celebration of how far the Tour has come over the years, an occasion when Beman and the tour professionals can stick out their chests with

Deane Beman has tried hard to get the TPC accepted as the fifth major. He enjoyed more success out of this sand trap.

pride. And no-one would begrudge them that, because the Tour is one of the great sporting success stories, and the venue sets impeccable standards, in the condition of the course, the practice facilities, and the way everyone in the Ponte Vedra community makes an effort. Captains of Florida industry and their wives, who live in the luxurious condos and houses that dot the complex, give up a week of their vacations to act as drivers to take the players and their wives anywhere they want to go. Everyone makes an effort.

The event began with Jack Nicklaus as the inaugural winner, and he did so in time-honored fashion, from three strokes off the lead with a round to play. The first three TPC's were played at various venues in the South, before moving to Sawgrass in 1977. The wind blew and no-one broke 70. Mark Hayes returned the winning 72-hole total, a score of 289, one over par. For the next three years Sawgrass played host and each year there was a quality champion: in order, Lanny Wadkins, Lee Trevino, and Raymond Floyd.

Jerry Takes a Dive

In 1982 the event moved for the final time to the players' own course, just across the road from Sawgrass. It was designed by Pete Dye and the initial reaction among the professionals was unfavorable, to say the least. Dye had a reputation for building exacting courses, and this was no exception. Still, he predicted a winning score of eight under, and when Jerry Pate came in with that exact total, he took home the Waterford crystal that goes to the winner. But first Pate dived into the lake that runs alongside the 18th, and earned heroic status among his fellow professionals by taking Beman and the demon Dye in with him.

Since then the event has been won by players who tend to be hot that year, rather than what happens in the majors, where the great competitors rise to the occasion. Hal Sutton, Fred Couples, Calvin Peete, and Tom Kite, to name but four of the last seven winners, all fit the mold. All were playing the best golf of their lives going into the TPC and all prevailed. It seems the elite players just cannot get motivated the way they are for the four major championships. That is one dilemma it is difficult to see how Beman can solve.

No-one could describe Jerry Pate as a shy boy. After winning the Players Championship in 1982, he dived into the nearby lake, taking Deane Beman and architect Pete Dye with him.

THE UNITED STATES AMATEUR CHAMPIONSHIP

The United States Amateur Championship officially began life 10 years after its British counterpart; both have retained their dignity, if not their influence over the golfing scene in their respective countries. In 1965, the U.S. Amateur flirted with a strokeplay format but, thankfully this lasted just eight years. There is a traditional link between matchplay and amateur golf, and thankfully the USGA recognized this before any lasting damage was done. When matchplay returned in 1973 the winner was a young man called Craig Stadler, of whom we would hear a great deal more.

The Merion course in Pennsylvania has seen many of the great moments in American golf and this tradition began in 1916 when Chick Evans became the first man to win the U.S. Open and Amateur in the same year. In that same event, a 14-year-old won two rounds before being knocked out. Not many people would defeat him when he was older: his name was Bobby Jones, and 14 years later he would repeat Evans' achievement, only this time double it, for he also won the two British legs of the Grand Slam as well. Astonishingly, the venue, once more, was Merion, and after it was all over, with no golf worlds left to conquer, Jones retired.

The Jones era of victories – there would be five in all – had begun at Merion six years earlier. It continued in 1927 and then a year later came a symbolic triumph. Here the United States champion was up against the British champion, T.P. Perkins. The initials of the British player did not stand for 'totally pulverized' but they may as well have. Perkins was beaten 10 & 9. He had had another dose of the Jones's. In the Walker Cup, Jones had beaten him 13 & 12, the biggest victory in the history of the event.

Sixty Three Hole Marathon

Before we leave the Jones era, there was another astonishing feat in the 1930

Winner of the US Amateur for the first time at the age of 38, Jay Sigel went on to conduct a successful defence.

Championship and that was by Maurice McCarthy. After tying for the last qualifying place, he won a play-off match the next morning that lasted 16 holes. Then followed a first round match that lasted 19 holes, and after that he went straight out again, and beat George von Elm but only at the 28th hole, the longest single round match in the history of the champion-

ship. In all, McCarthy had played 63 holes in one day.

After World War II, the Amateur grew as never before. Each year there seemed to be record fields with the entrants reaching 1,600 in 1956. Two years earlier one name in particular had stood out. The winner was Arnold Palmer. In 1959, another man who would go on to greater things, Jack

Tom Kite was pipped for the 1970 US Amateur title by Lanny Wadkins. As his professional career unfolded this proved to be a story that would repeat itself time and again.

Nicklaus, became the second youngest winner of the event. Two years later Nicklaus would win again, and then he turned professional. His first win in that arena was the 1962 U.S. Open.

The man who separated the Nicklaus triumphs was Deane Beman, one of the finest putters of his time, who would also win the event on two occasions. Like Nicklaus, Beman's influence is still felt to date as U.S. tour commissioner.

The one notable winner of the stroke-play years was Lanny Wadkins, who in a vintage finish to the 1970 Amateur edged out Tom Kite. Wadkins's total of 279 was the lowest during these unsettling years.

The Road to Success

By now, the fields for the event had grown beyond the 2,500 mark and, not surprisingly, such strong entry lists produced quality champions. After Stadler, there was Jerry Pate, and after Pate there was Mark O'Meara, then John Cook, and finally Hal Sutton.

It was a remarkable run for all these players would go on to win tournaments on the pro tour, and become millionaires. Clearly winning the Amateur was a prelude to professional success but occasionally it was nothing more

than that. In 1978, there was one of the great sentimental victories when Bing Crosby's son Nathaniel triumphed at the 37th hole of a final in which he had been three down with seven to play. The venue was the Olympic club in San Francisco, just a few miles from the Crosby home. Nathaniel turned professional, but with no great success. In 1982, Jay Sigel, one of the greatest amateurs in the world over the last 25 years or so, won his first title at his 16th attempt. The venue was The Country Club and at 38 he was the oldest winner for 14 years. Twelve months on and having taken so long to win it, Sigel showed no inclination to relinquish the trophy. From an entry of 3,553, he successfully defended, the first man to do so since Harvie Ward in 1955-6.

THE U.S. MASTERS

The burgeoning interest in golf is never more vividly expressed than in the continuing growth of early season tournaments, but for all the expansion, the Masters remains the definitive Ode to Spring, the signal for players of all abilities in the Northern Hemisphere once more to fall under the spell of the Royal and Ancient game. In Europe the reputation of the Masters stands even higher than in its native land, for most Americans would cite the United States Open as the most important of the three major championships played every year in the New World.

On the other side of the Atlantic, the Masters is held in the sort of reverence the U.S. Open has never come close to capturing. For millions in Europe, those late nights in the early days of April have assumed a significance far beyond the playing of the tournament. Television is relaying its first golf event of the year: it means the winter is over, and now to be enjoyed are the most glorious of the four seasons.

'What does winning the Masters mean? Jeepers, its the world!' exclaimed Nick Faldo after slipping on the famous green jacket, and then he recounted the tale of how he had stayed up as a 13-year-old to watch the 1971 event relayed from Augusta.

The Masters is special too because of the course it is played on. The floral splendor of Augusta is dealt with in detail elsewhere, so suffice it to say that of all the envious eyes that are cast on a golf correspondent's lot, none are anything like as green as when he is packing his or her bag to head for Augusta. For in April, Georgia is on every golfer's mind.

An Invitational Event

The event is the only one to be played on the same course each year, thus adding to the Augusta mystique, and it is the newest of the four major championships. When Bobby Jones, the greatest amateur of them all retired in 1930, the Grand Slam he had achieved that year consisted of the Amateur and the Open

They still talk about Gene Sarazen's albatross in the 1935 Masters. Forty six years later he was searching for similar inspiration.

championships of Great Britain and America. Little could he have known that he himself would have a leading say in changing that tradition. At the start, the last thing on Jones's mind was to create a tournament that would acquire such stature. Jones imagined and conceived Augusta as a place where he could invite all his golfing friends and so he did in 1934. He called the tournament the Augusta National Invitation, and Jones was so loved by his peers that they cherished visiting him. But Jones had it all wrong with regard to the event's title. It did not last the week, as newspapermen quickly dubbed it The Masters. And so the extraordinary deeds that the course and the event had inspired over the years began. In 1935 Gene Sarazen holed a 4-wood second shot on the 15th for an albatross (or double eagle) which ultimately led him to tie, and then defeat in a sudden death play-off, Craig Wood. It is no coincidence that the Masters, in a relatively short period of time, has accumulated a catalogue of extraordinary drama. The course is one of immaculate design, with the back nine built to glorify the worthy and expose the pretenders.

Despite its major status, the Masters remains an invitation event, and the championship committee have resolutely resisted worldwide pressure for change. They argue that they never sought such a position of eminence, although this smacks these days of false modesty. And so the field is always a great deal less in number than those for the other three major events, and its criteria for invitation does include some oddball categories dating back to the days when amateur golf held a position of influence infinitely greater than it does today.

At Augusta, you never see advertising billboards. There is no massive roadshow that has to be staged to make the event viable. The whims of exhibitors or corporate sponsors do not have to be taken into account either, simply because there are none. For all these absentees, much thanks. The Masters generates its income from patron's badges which go out to the same people every year. Because the attendance is limited to around 25,000 a day, these badges have become one of the most prized possessions in sport,

and during tournament week legion are the people outside on Washington Road holding up signs saying: 'Masters tickets wanted.'

They are not the only images of sadness the Masters has created. None was sadder than Roberto de Vicenzo when he lost the 1968 Masters for the most heartbreaking of all reasons. That year the most gentlemanly of golfer had appeared to tie with Bob Goalby only to be told that he had signed for a four at the 17th instead of a three, and his 65 had been irrevocably recorded as a 66. He had 'lost' by one shot, and not even at the Masters, do they dare change the rules of golf. No-one ever suffered a more poignant 45th birthday; but typically the Argentine never wallowed in self-pity. 'What a stupid I am' he said at a characteristically courteous press conference.

As you would expect, the Masters' tradition is inextricably tied up with the great names of golf. In the 1950s Ben Hogan and Sam Snead brought the best out of one another during a six year spell, the former won the event twice and the latter three times. Hogan laid down some ground rules for playing the back nine. He always aimed short and to the right of the treacherous 11th green, declaring: 'If you ever see me hit the 11th green in two, it means I have mishit my second shot.' Larry Mize, although inadvertently, showed the wisdom of this philosophy in the play-off for the 1987 Masters, when he chipped in from 50 feet to the right of the green for a birdie to defeat Greg Norman. Nor did Hogan go for the green in two at the par fives, the 13th or 15th, a policy that would get him castigated for caution in these days of high-tech equipment. Not that the ice-man would have cared, although with all the improvements in technique and

equipment, it is feasible he would have thought differently these days.

Hogan also started the tradition whereby the winner pays for and hosts a champions' dinner when the ensemble gather at Augusta the following Spring. He even gets to choose the menu although those gathered in 1989 pondered the wisdom of this when Sandy Lyle specified the notorious, if traditional, Scottish dish of haggis, neeps and tatties.

Master of The Masters

In the 60s, the dominant figures were Jack Nicklaus and Arnold Palmer to the extent that no other player donned a green jacket for six years. Palmer won his two titles with typical panache, birdieing the last hole on each occasion. Nicklaus went on to add three more to the three he won during that decade, and his total of six is a record that will stand for some time yet, if not in perpetuity. The last of his wins, in 1986, was perhaps the most emotional of all the 54 Masters that have been held to date. The week began with him being written off in the Atlanta Constitution. Nicklaus seethed when he saw the article to the extent that he cut it out and stuck it on the refrigerator door of the house he and his family had rented out for the week. 'Just to motivate me if I ever feel a little lack-luster this week.'

Jack looked pretty lack-luster with 11 holes to play. He was not even on the leaderboard. Then came one of those charges that, over two generations, have shaken even players who look unshakable, in this instance it was Severiano Ballesteros. The Masters chairman, Hord Hardin, said afterwards he was worried about subsequent Masters events because –

Two of the great moments in Masters history. Jack Nicklaus (left) sinks a birdie putt at the 17th and the delight on his face illustrates his belief that a sixth Augusta success was within his grasp. Delight for Sandy Lyle too (right) as he becomes the first ever British winner.

well, how do you come up with an encore after that? He need not have creased his brow. First there was that chip-in from the hometown boy Mize, who used to peek at Augusta from over the boundary wall.

Then there was Sandy Lyle's win following what has been described as the greatest bunker shot of all time. Next it was Faldo's turn and suddenly the event that non-Americans found the most difficult to win was turning into a European convention. Before 1980, when Ballesteros became the youngest champion, the South African Gary Player was the only overseas competitor to have won. In the 80s there were no less than five European triumphs. So, with its insatiable appetite for intrigue and excitement, the Masters will go on thrilling us all, and 13-year-olds in Europe will continue to stay up late at night and dream of doing what Faldo did, and turning that dream into reality.

Faldo's 35ft birdie putt on the second extra hole of a play-off against Scott Hoch disappears and realization dawns – he is the champion.

THE UNITED STATES OPEN

The United States Golf Association has come in for a deal of criticism for the way the courses they use are 'doctored' for play in the United States Open. There is a body of professional opinion that argues that their uniform design of stringent rough, narrow fairways, and putting surfaces guarded by impenetrable rough takes the edge off the skills of the shotmaker and explains a number of what the detractors consider unworthy winners over the years.

Whatever the merits of this argument, it does not hold water alongside the stature of the three men who have won most Opens in the modern era. The total stands at four wins, and it is held by three Americans who, in the judgement of many, are the greatest players in the history of golf: Bobby Jones, Ben Hogan, and Jack Nicklaus.

Early Years

The U.S. Open began life in 1895 and, like its elder brother, the British Open, it was dominated in the early years by British golfers, for the very simple reason that few other people played the game. The event first assumed national significance with the 1913 event at The Country Club in Brookline, Massachusetts. The greatest British players of the day had hardly bothered with the event. Indeed Harry Vardon's win in the 1900 Open came about only because he was in the country at the time playing exhibition golf. But for the 1913 Open he and Ted Ray had gathered in Boston and after 72 holes the pair had finished in a tie with a young man from Brookline named Francis Ouimet. A good amateur, but nothing more than that, at least up to that point, Ouimet had almost withdrawn on the eve of the event because he feared he would humiliate himself after two depressing practice rounds of 88 strokes each. But although he had not been given a ghost of a chance in the play-off, he wrote a unique page in history for himself by defeating his two English rivals.

'The shots heard round the world' was how Ouimet's triumph was herald-

Francis Ouimet's victory in the 1913 US Open ushered in an era of American domination of golf that lasted until the 1980s.

ed, because it proved that at last America had a player who could stand alongside the best of the British. That win marked the starting point of well-nigh 70 years' domination of the game by American players, and its significance was recognized by the USGA who returned to The Country Club on both the 50th and 75th anniversaries. And you can guarantee they will be back in 2013.

There have been occasional British successes to salute but they have been isolated affairs. Ray's win in 1920 was a milestone for other reasons. Ridiculous as it seems now, up to that point (and, it has to be said, for a good many years after in golf's mother-country) professionals were looked upon as some form of sub-species and not allowed into the clubhouse. That all

changed in Ray's year, and once the precedent had been set, such obnoxious snobbery was swept away with it. In recognition of the part the emancipators, the Inverness club in Ohio, had played, the professionals led by Water Hagen, donated a clock which still graces the clubhouse.

Playing by the Rules

In 1925 Bobby Jones set the sort of standard in sportsmanship that characterized his life, and which has been upheld in golf ever since. He called a penalty shot on himself that no-one else had seen, and when he was later congratulated on the act, he said: 'You might as well praise a man for not robbing a bank.'

Jones won the first of his titles the

'so tough that nobody can win.' For that reason, Hogan regards his last round of 67 as the finest he ever played and with evident satisfaction he told the gathering at the prize-giving ceremony: 'I am glad to have brought the monster to its knees.'

Thus Hogan had successfully defended his title, a feat that subsequently proved beyond everyone until Curtis Strange in 1988 and 1989. By contrast, when Hogan won for a fourth time in 1953, who else could have been second but the eternal Open nearly man, Snead?

Whereas Hogan's and, indeed, Jones's victories were achieved over a short space of time, the same cannot be said about Jack Nicklaus's. Hogan himself had witnessed the first coming of Nicklaus in 1960. The winner that year, for the only time, was Arnold Palmer, but Hogan sat in the clubhouse after playing with the then chubby, rather than Golden, Bear, and said: 'I have just played with a kid who should have won this event by ten shots.' No-one took much notice at the time. Palmer had won as only Palmer

---

Champions come no more popular than these two. All the grace and power of Bobby Jones (left) is shown in this scene from his fourth US Open win. Fuzzy Zoeller (below) was no stylist by comparison but his 1984 play-off win over Greg Norman was Jones-like in its sportsmanship.

following year, and between 1927 and 1930 won both the British Open twice and U.S. Open three times.

While the Open trophy is graced by great names, there is one missing, and it is to Sam Snead's everlasting regret that his record number of tour victories does not include his national championship. He should have won one, maybe two, but then perhaps every man should have a regret to niggle him.

The Hogan Era

Snead lost a play-off in 1947 but then came the Ben Hogan era when the greatest shot-maker the game has known won four titles in the next six years. The most emotional of these has been dealt with elsewhere, for it is irrevocably wrapped up in the history of one club, Merion. Then Hogan was still recovering from a horrific car accident that had left his life hanging by a thread. A year on, in 1951 at Oakland Hills, even one with so consummate an approach as Hogan was shocked by what he saw. So penal was the Michigan course that one member declared it

As the eighties drew to a close so Curtis Strange established himself among the game's upper echelons with two consecutive victories in the US Open in 1988 and '89.

could win. Six birdies in the first seven holes led to a fabulous 65, and victory over Nicklaus by two shots. Subsequently, Nicklaus, who was an amateur at the time, achieved the startling feat of making his first professional victory his first major championship win as well, taking the Open at Oakmont two years later. It would be 18 years before Nicklaus would equal the record of four before an emotional gathering at Baltusrol, the scene of his second win as well in 1967.

In the interim there were four runner-up spots, most notably at Pebble Beach in 1982. Nicklaus had won his third Open there a decade earlier but now he was undone by one of the truly

great shots in Open history, as Tom Watson chipped in from a desperate position on the next to last hole.

Heroic Deeds

In 1964, there was a victory for Ken Venturi which even matched for sheer bravery that of Hogan at Merion. Like Hogan, Venturi had to overcome crippling disability. Over the preceding years, he had been plagued by back injuries and illness, and a circulatory problem had led to him losing some sense of feel in his hand. The venue, Congressional in Washington, was afflicted by oppressive humidity, and to add to Venturi's list of problems, he suffered dehydration as well. Just to complete the picture, there was mental anguish. Venturi had lost three Masters titles in previous years in the most heartbreaking of circumstances. Now he put all that behind him. 'Beware

the injured golfer' goes the cliché and maybe it was Venturi's example that inspired it. When he walked down the last fairway there was not a dry eye in the house. As he holed out, he muttered through the tears: 'My God, I have won the Open.'

Since then, there have been some truly heroic deeds. There were two wins for Lee Trevino, and even one for a British golfer, in 1970, when Tony Jacklin became the first Briton since Ray at Inverness precisely fifty years earlier. Three years later, Johnny Miller won at Oakmont with a spellbinding last round 63. In 1976 the Open went to the Deep South for the first time, and Atlanta Athletic Club responded not only by setting new attendance records but also by conjuring a sensational finish with a scarcely credible 5-iron on the closing hole from thick rough over water to two feet by Jerry Pate. If ever one shot deserved to win the Open it was that one.

And so it continued into the 80s, with memorable wins for Watson, Fuzzy Zoeller, and Strange's back-to-back triumphs. Yes, as the detractors claim, there has been the odd dodgy winner, a player perhaps not worthy to mention in the same breath as the great ones. But with its centenary in sight, the USGA can look back at a glorious and significant slice of golfing history.

Hale Irwin used to be a top-class athlete and even at 45 he can still run rings round the 18th green at Medinah. He did have something to celebrate, the holing of an enormous putt that prefaced his play-off victory.

THE U.S. PGA CHAMPIONSHIP

The poignant sight of golfer Mike Reid succumbing to the pressure of the occasion in the 1989 U.S. PGA surely removed any doubts that this tournament remains one of the four major championships. Reid, who had been playing relentlessly accurate golf, finished bogey, double bogey, par, to lose the event to Payne Stewart; and the enormity of his failure so overcame him at the press conference afterwards that he broke down seven times. Jack Nicklaus told him in the locker room: 'I have never felt so bad for anyone. You played too well to lose.' There are some who try to knock the PGA, but does that flood of emotion from a 30-year-old trying to leave his thumbprint on history, or those consoling words from a legend who knew what a cruel trick fate had played on Reid, sound to you like reactions to a run-of-the-mill tour event?

It is important to keep this all in perspective. At various times over the past 20 years, the World Series, the World Matchplay Championship, the Memorial Tournament, and the Players' Championship have all had their supporters (usually with vested interests) attempting to have them classified as major championships. Thankfully, all have failed. Tradition has decreed us four majors, and it is enough. And the fourth of these in every sense, is the PGA Championship.

Hagen's Four in a Row

It began life as a matchplay event in 1916, and there are many who argue that it was through changing the format to strokeplay in 1958 that the event lost some of its appeal. It certainly lost its uniqueness. The first great PGA champion was Walter Hagen who set the record (since equalled by Jack Nicklaus) of five wins but one of the best early occasions was the year he lost in the final. His opponent in 1923 was Gene Sarazen, and Hagen was two down with three to play. He then dis-

played the strength of mind that was such a factor behind his imperious matchplay record, winning both the next two holes. The last of the 36 holes was halved, and so the final went into extra-time. At the second extra hole, it appeared Hagen's title as Sarazen was hopelessly wayward off the tee. From a seemingly impossible spot however, he conjured a wonderful recovery shot, which finished two feet from the flag. A startled Hagen could only find a bunker with his approach, and Sarazen had successfully defended his title. There was to be no hat-trick of victories (though Sarazen would win again 10 years later). The next four PGA Championships were all won by the flamboyant Hagen, and he remains the only 20th century golfer to have won a major four times in a row. It will be something of a sensation if that re-cord is equalled before, or for that matter, after, the Millenium.

Hagen's attempt to win a fifth title in succession ended in ignominy. He was thrashed 6 & 5 by Leo Diegel in the semi-finals, and after the victor had gone on to beat Al Espinosa in the final, Hagen told Diegel there was no trophy for him because he had lost it. He said he had left it in the back of a taxi. Some months later it was discovered in the Chicago offices of Hagen's clubmakers.

The Nelson Touch

During the War years, Byron Nelson dominated. In six years he reached the final five times, losing three of them on the 36th, 37th and 38th greens. His 1945 win over Sam Byrd will always be remembered, however, for it was part of a quite staggering sequence of 11 successive tournament victories (all told, he won 18 times that year).

The PGA Championship was enjoying some halcyon days. Ben Hogan won the title twice in 1946 and 1948, his great rival Sam Snead in 1949 and 1951. But storm clouds that would plague it for 20 years were soon to disturb the tranquillity. In 1953, Ben Hogan opted out of the championship and

A rare picture of Walter Hagen minus plus fours. It was rare too when he did not make at least the final of the U.S. PGA in the early years.

In the 1940s no-one could touch Byron Nelson. He reached the final of the then matchplay event on five occasions out of six. Even in later years, he still possessed a mean short game.

went instead to play in the British Open at Carnoustie. While Hogan was writing his name on the oldest piece of silverware, the PGA was won by a journeyman professional called Walter Burkemo. The following year the event went to Chick Harbert.

The U.S. PGA is run by the PGA of America, whose main task is to cater for the welfare of club professionals. Clearly there was a conflict of interest here, since the tournament by now had become an event that should be contested by tournament pros. To this day, the PGA has dragged its feet on the issue. There are still too many club pros playing in the event (one of the reasons for its loss of luster) but back in the 50s, the situation was still more farcical.

Events were now drawing to a head. Television was not thrilled by finals such as that of Harbert against Burkemo, and in 1958, the change to the strokeplay format was made. Despite the low-key finals, there were many who considered the PGA would lose everything by conforming. But the main problem in the years that followed had little to do with the change to strokeplay. The problems were that the continued preponderance of club professionals; the fact that the event was played in the same month as the British Open; and the standard of courses the event was taken to.

Not for the first time, Nicklaus succinctly summed up the problem. He said: 'The PGA is killing its own tournament. The British Open is a major tournament and scheduling the PGA right behind it in July is not very smart. All the players would like to see the PGA be a better tournament than it is, but it won't be if it is going to be scheduled this way, and if we continue to make golf courses by playing the PGA on them, instead of playing the PGA on famous courses.'

If Arnold Palmer can be said to be the saviour of the British Open, then perhaps a similar role can be assigned to Nicklaus in the PGA. His criticisms were taken to heart, and in the years that followed, the event was held at such grand venues as Inverness, Congressional, Oakland Hills, Oakmont, and Pebble Beach.

There are no gaps in Jack's honors board — he dominated the U.S. PGA like he did the other majors. His five wins equals Hagen's record.

The instigation in 1974 of the players' own event, the Tournament Players' Championship, has never really constituted the threat to the PGA some would have us believe. And the 80s saw the PGA reclaim some of its prestige, and re-establish itself as one of the four majors. In 1984, the event was poignantly dominated by two vete-rans, with Lee Trevino scoring four rounds in the 60s to outstrip Gary Player.

Tway Hooks the Shark

Two years later at Inverness, Ohio, Bob Tway holed out from a bunker on the 72nd hole to defeat Greg Norman. It was the most dramatic of shots, and the sense of occasion was heightened

The U.S. PGA has had its fair share of drama in recent years. Bob Tway (left) is exultant after a holed bunker shot ensured him victory in 1986 while the hangman's noose (below) failed to bother the 1988 winner Jeff Sluman, anymore than the bunker in which he found himself.

by the fact that Norman going into the final round had been in the lead, just as he had in every other major played that year.

The vast majority of players approach the PGA in a way they adopt for only three other tournaments each year. The ones with their heads out of the dollar bag know that it represents one of their four chances each year to secure immortality, the final recognition that in the world of golf, they are somebody special. That is why players who lose in heartrending circumstances get words of consolation from Nicklaus. And why the players themselves indulge in a tear or two, whether they be of joy or sadness.

Payne Stewart breezed into the Windy City in 1989 and found favor with the locals on the last day by wearing the colors of the Bears. They were able to cheer on a 'home' victory too as the colourful Stewart claimed his first major championship.

THE U.S. WOMEN'S OPEN

There are now women professional golfers all over the globe, but for the most adept it is a case of: Go West, Young Woman. Their destination is the Ladies' Professional Golf Association circuit of America. It has become one of the great success stories of the post-war years, with prize money spiralling from $45,000 in 1950 to beyond $12 million in 1990. And the most important event on the tour is the United States Women's Open. It began in 1946 and was adopted by the United States Golf Association in 1950. Like the U.S. GA's other events, such as the Open, this one remains free of corporate sponsorship influence, although its importance is recognized by the general public wherever it is played. The event is televised live by one of the network American television stations, but even so it is not unusual to see crowds of 15,000 watching each day's play. It offers by no means the biggest purse on the LPGA tour, but some events are beyond money and this is one of them. Its prestige extends way beyond the things that mere dollars can buy.

Rather like the men's PGA, this major championship began life as a matchplay event, but that lasted just one year. The early years were dominated by two of the great names of women's golf – Mildred 'Babe' Zaharias, and Louise Suggs.

At the request of the LPGA, the U.S.GA took charge of running the event in 1953 and they attracted a field of 37, of whom 17 were professionals. In 1954, Zaharias, in her last appearance, won for the third time by no less than 12 shots. It was the most poignant of victories. Twelve months earlier, she had been undergoing an operation for cancer. Not surprisingly, given the manner of her triumph, it was compared to Ben Hogan's Open victory at Merion 12 months on from his near-fatal car crash.

This is the face that has melted a thousand hearts but the U.S. Open still eludes Nancy Lopez.

The Wright Stuff

If Zaharias's last victory was heart-rending, then Betsy Rawls's in 1957 was heartbreaking. She claimed her third title without actually returning the lowest score. That belonged to Jacqueline Pung, but it was discovered she had signed for a five at the 4th instead of a six. Although the overall total was correct, and the mistake her marker's, Pung was disqualified because a player is solely responsible for his or her score at each individual hole. Had the mistake been in the addition, it would not have mattered. The members of Winged Foot, the venue, were mortified that such a sporting tragedy could happen at their course. They promptly raised a collection, which reached in excess of $3,000. It was a magnificent gesture, particularly in the light of a first prize of $1,800. Pung, who had lost a play-off to Rawls for the 1953 title, was never to win the event, for the years that followed belonged to Mickey Wright, arguably the greatest woman golfer in history, who would win it four times out of the next six events in which she competed.

In 1967, there was a rare overseas winner – and a famous one at that. Over the Cascades course, in Hot Springs, Virginia, Catherine Lacoste, daughter of the legendary French tennis player René, won by two strokes from Susie Maxwell and Beth Stone. It was the first, and to date, only triumph in the event by an amateur. Catherine's mother, then Simone Thion de la Chaume, had won the Ladies British Open Amateur title in 1927.

Another amateur made her mark in the 1975 Open won, by Sandra Palmer. Among those tied for second place was a very young Nancy Lopez. Astonishingly, in view of that precocious performance, and her later achievements, she is still awaiting her first Open title. In the 80s, there were no dominant players in the event, indicating the strength in depth that is prevalent in women's golf. The growth of the game worldwide was indicated in successive victories for European players, Laura Davies from England, and Liselotte Neumann from Sweden, although the decade closed on a success for the American Betsy King. King proved the queen of women's golf that year. She also topped the money list with $654,000 earned. No wonder the young women of today continue to go west.

Betsy King proved the queen of women's golf in 1989. Her US Open win was the crowning moment.

THE WALKER CUP

The Walker Cup takes its name from George Walker, President of the United States Golf Association, who, in 1920, offered to donate a trophy for a challenge match involving all countries who wished to dispatch an amateur team to the United States. If you've ever thrown a party and worried that no-one would turn up, then you will get some idea how Walker felt when every single nation turned down his invitation.

Desperate for competition, the Americans decided that if the world was not going to come to them, they would go to the world. Or, more specifically, England, where an élite eight-man amateur team that included past or future Open champions Francis Ouimet, Chick Evans and Bobby Jones soundly defeated a British team by nine mat-

There were high hopes for the British Walker Cup team in 1988 at Sunningdale but Jay Sigel (center) and his colleagues had no trouble maintaining American dominance of the event.

ches to three on the eve of the 1921 British Amateur Championship.

This, then, was the forerunner of the Walker Cup, which was played for the first time the following year. It was a taste of what was to come in every sense. To date, Great Britain and Ireland has won just four of the 32 matches played against the United States.

Among the press covering a lowly team in any sport, there is a hoary old joke along the lines that if you turn up early enough the danger is they will give you a game. In 1922, that turned out to be the case. The British captain, Robert Harris, fell ill, and Bernard Darwin, sent to the National Golf Links, New York, to cover the match for *The Times*, played twice, winning his single. It was not the last time a writer was to have an influence on the trophy. In 1932, Leonard Crawley's influence was directly on the cup itself, when his 5-iron shot to the 18th green sailed over the target. Without a bounce, it smashed into the trophy, causing a dent. Later to become golf correspon-

dent for *The Daily Telegraph*, Crawley was saved from embarrassment by the fact that he was the only Briton to gain a point at The Country Club that year.

And that was the way of it in the early years. In the first match in Britain in 1923, there was but a point between the teams. After that the contest became a biennial one and British hopes a forlorn one. In 1926, Jones defeated Cyril Tolley by 12 & 11. Two years later in Chicago, Jones beat Phil Perkins 13 & 12. But then, Jones would have beaten anyone.

British encouragement was restricted to individual performances, but then, after the ignominy of losing by $1\frac{1}{2}$-$10\frac{1}{2}$ at Pine Valley in 1936, they went from their worst result to their best, winning at St. Andrews for the first time two years later. The only other British victory on home soil was also at St. Andrews, but the two matches spanned an interval of no less than 33 years. In any case, no-one should assume that a visit to the Home of Golf reduces Americans to a state of awe.

Jay Sigel drives off first in his singles match against Bobby Eggo in 1988 (top) and he was still in front come the end of the match; better times for Great Britain and Ireland two years later (below) as Craig Cassells leads the victory celebrations.

The match has been played over the Old Course a total of eight times, and has led in the main to some thumping American wins.

Sixty-Seven Year Wait

In between those two British successes, the only thing that stopped the Americans was World War II and a halved match in 1965 at Five Farms, Baltimore, where Britain won six of the eight singles on the first day and were dreaming of a first-ever success on American soil when they led convincingly at the halfway stage. But the home team staged a dramatic recovery on the final afternoon. Indeed it needed Clive Clark to hole a wonderful 30ft putt to prevent Britain stumbling to another defeat.

But the British would eventually win on American soil, even if they did have to wait 67 years for it to happen. The venue was Peachtree, Atlanta, in 1989. Like the win in 1938, this victory followed humiliating defeat two years earlier, and like Baltimore in 1965 it looked for long periods on the final day as if GB&I were going to throw away a convincing first-day advantage. But the visitors were not to be denied on this occasion. Jim Milligan secured victory in the most heroic of circumstances, when, the last man out on the course against the formidable Walker Cup veteran Jay Sigel, he came from two down with three to play to win each of the final holes and so secure the narrowest of $12\frac{1}{2}$-$11\frac{1}{2}$ wins. Portmarnock in September 1991 will give a better idea if this is a temporary blockage in the flow of American victories or whether the Walker Cup has truly entered a new era.

THE WESTERN OPEN

The Western Open is the oldest event on the United States tour and in keeping with its long and proud tradition it was also one of the last to sell out to corporate sponsorship. If there had been a professional Grand Slam 40 years ago then the Western Open would have been part of it. But in the face of today's big-money events, its status declined, and it is only since accepting the mighty dollar of big business – it is now the Centel Western Open – that it has been able to compete once more on even terms with today's $1 million-plus tournaments.

It was first held in 1899 and among the early winners were those great Scots, Laurie Auchterlonie and Willie Smith. Since then every American professional who ever aspired to the game's élite bracket has written his name at some time or other on to the Western Open winner's board. Walter Hagen did so on no less than five separate occasions, while in recent years Tom Watson won it three times. In addition some non-professionals have been successful as well, including Chick Evans in 1910. Six years later he would become the first man to win both the U.S. Amateur and Open titles in the same season.

Just as startling a triumph was registered by Scott Verplank in 1985, when he became the first amateur to win a Tour event since Gene Littler in 1954. Moreover, Verplank won the event the hard way, at the second extra hole of a sudden death play-off against Jim Thorpe. Of almost equal value in the surprise, not to mention record book stakes, was Jim Benepe's triumph in 1988. Benepe, a graduate from Northwestern University in 1986, was competing in his first tour event, and looked to be heading for second place with Peter Jacobsen needing a par four at the last to win. Benepe was thrilled at the prospect of the runner's up spot – in his shoes who wouldn't be? – but Jacobsen was to give him cause for further celebration when he found the water with his approach shot and contrived to register a double bogey six. The last player to win his first Tour event was Ben Crenshaw in the 1973 San Antonio Texas Open.

Laurie Auchterlonie, an early Western winner.

THE WORLD CUP

The World Cup was started with the intention of fostering goodwill between golf-playing nations, but in recent times the event itself has found it hard to attract the top players or to find a suitable date on the increasingly crowded calendar of world golf.

The players managed by the Mark McCormack organisation (the International Management Group) have largely given it a miss, which has prompted dark whisperings that it is because the same group runs the rival event, the Dunhill Nations Cup. The European Tour's Executive Director Ken Schofield says that such people are putting one and one together and getting three. 'Can you prove that such workings are going on, because if you can I would like to see the evidence,' he told one reporter.

Way back in an altogether more innocent world, the American industrialist John Jay Hopkins felt the sport was ready for a team competition involving all nations, and not just the two involved in the Ryder Cup. In 1953, he launched the Canada Cup, with two-man teams invited to represent their country in Montreal. The Argentine team of Roberto de Vicenzo and Antonio Cerda were the first winners. Since then the United States has proved the overwhelming power, winning the event six years out of seven at one stage. As their team invariably contained either Jack Nicklaus or Arnold Palmer and sometimes both, it was hardly surprising. The event went to the far corners of the globe and was played on some superb courses that might otherwise have remained unrecognized. The Jockey Club in Argentina and Kasumigaseki in Japan are just two such examples.

The title was changed to the World Cup in 1967, but these days it carries none of the prestige of soccer's event of the same name. As it withered into decline in the 80s, so McCormack began the Dunhill Cup, only for the Philip Morris Group to pump some money and some life back into the World Cup. The problem for the event now is not just McCormack's event, but the great proliferation of other team events, plus of course the ever-increasing demands imposed on the top players to appear all over the world.

The World Cup set out with the ideal of promoting fellowship through golf and the Australian pairing of Peter Fowler and Wayne Grady were certainly in the mood to show goodwill to all men after their 1989 win.

THE WORLD MATCHPLAY CHAMPIONSHIP

If the Masters at Augusta in April is the definitive springtime date, then (for British hearts at least) the World Matchplay Championship is the Ode to Autumn. When Wentworth's leaves turn all the shades of brown and gold, all minds center on the West course for the annual roller-coaster ride containing all the unpredictable excitement that matchplay golf can bring.

The worldwide boom in the sport has precipitated a decline in international status for the event, but it remains a pioneering concept, and second only to the British Open Championship itself in the affections of its British audience. It could have asked for no better first winner than Arnold Palmer in 1964, and in each of the 27 events that have followed the full gamut of human emotions have been expressed. The 36-hole format encourages adventurous play. There has been some mesmerizing scoring and no more so than in 1986, when Tommy Nakajima went round in a morning seven-under-par 65, and an afternoon 64, yet still lost on the 38th hole to Sandy Lyle.

The World Matchplay Championship was the brainchild of Mark McCormack. The name of the tournament was alluring, a sponsor was found, and since McCormack managed just about every golfer who was worth managing, a top-class field was ensured. The event got off to the sort of start that makes reputations. In the semi-finals there was a slice of vintage Palmer. He began with an eagle, a par, and four birdies against Gary Player and was five up after six holes. He went on to win by 8 & 6. A redoubtable performance by Neil Coles in the other half of the draw ensured the ideal first final; the biggest name in the sport against a player from the host country. Palmer won by 2 & 1, and that would be the way of it for British players for 22 years.

The Player Years

The 36-hole format suited the swashbuckling Palmer perfectly, but if ever one man was born to play matchplay golf it was Player. Matchplay golf is a game of wits, where one man's will is pitted against another's. No-one was stronger willed than the South African Player. He would dominate the event, winning five times in the next nine

---

The World Matchplay Championship was the perfect vehicle for the tenacious skills of Gary Player, and he duly won it on five separate occasions.

years on a course that, ideally speaking, favors the longer hitters off the tee. Rather than being intimidated by such a disadvantage, Player was inspired. In 1965 he defeated Palmer in the semifinals and the Open champion Peter Thomson in the final. But the match that is always remembered is an earlier victory over Tony Lema.

Champagne Tony, as he was known,

must have imbibed a glass or two of his favorite tipple over lunch. At all events, with nine holes to play, he was five up on Player, and a repeat of the thrashing Player had suffered a year earlier at the hands of Palmer appeared on the cards. Such a thought never crossed Player's mind. Neither did merely making the final losing margin 'respectable.' He still thought he could win. And so he did, clawing back Lema's advantage and winning at the first extra hole. A year later he successfully defended his title by knocking out Palmer again at the semi-final stage, and Jack Nicklaus by 6 & 4 in the final.

These were vintage years for an event that had gripped the imagination of the public. All the great names showed up, and when Player allowed them a chance, they all wrote their names on the trophy. Palmer won again in 1967, the left-hander Bob Charles in 1969, and Nicklaus (over Lee Trevino) in 1970.

In the 1972 semi-finals Trevino met Tony Jacklin just three months after he had beaten him in the British Open championship at Muirfield. The chance had therefore presented itself for Jacklin to exact some sort of revenge. Certainly that was how it was billed and the audience who turned up caught the mood and also the belief that, if Jacklin prevailed, there was every chance of the first British winner in the event. Well, Jacklin went round in 63 in the afternoon, and even in this event that has never been bettered. The match went every inch of its scheduled 36 holes, but at the end it was Trevino's arms who were once more held high in celebration. Jacklin, four down at lunch, had left himself with too much to do against a player performing pretty close to the peak of his powers as well. Later, Jacklin, winner of the British and US Open Championships, would describe it as the 'finest golf of my life.' Just to gall him further, Trevi-

Lee Trevino won the British Open in 1972 and after a momentous victory over Tony Jacklin, had high hopes of adding the World Matchplay. But it was Tom Weiskopf who prevailed in the final.

Above: On the 2nd, Ian Woosnam attempts a birdie putt but it stayed out and it was Nick Faldo who went on to win this final in 1989. Left: Sandy Lyle plays out of a bunker during the 1987 tournament won by Woosnam.

no could not reproduce the same result in the final, and lost to Tom Weiskopf.

In the mid-70s there were wins for Australians David Graham and Graham Marsh in successive years, and back-to-back victories for Hale Irwin.

If the early years belonged to Player, then the 80s went to the tournament's second dominant personality, Severiano Ballesteros. He would win it four times out of five from 1981 and invariably the finals would be close, exciting affairs. In 1981 he won by one hole over Ben Crenshaw, a year later it was at the 37th against Sandy Lyle. When Bal-

lesteros did not win, it was Greg Norman (in 1980, 1983, and 1986) who did. On each occasion he defeated a British golfer in the final, and it appeared that a British golfer would never win.

Britons on the Board

As the decade reached its close, however, the tournament found it increasingly hard to attract the best overseas, or more specifically, American, players. The non-appearance of some Americans was undoubtedly a factor in the recent British domination of the event,

although the plain fact is that Faldo, Ballesteros, Lyle (at his best) and Ian Woosnam are a match for the Americans (or anyone else) at Wentworth these days.

In the last three years of the 80s, the three Britons took turns to win. In 1987 it was Woosnam over Lyle; a year later, Lyle beat Faldo, after thrashing Ballesteros by the indecent margin of 7 & 6 in the semi-final; and then in 1989 Faldo beat Woosnam. The 1990s began with another Woosnam win. This time the Welshman triumphed over Zimbabwean, Mark McNulty.

Such finals of course ensured that the British audiences remained faithful, in terms of both television figures, and actual attendance on the course. But, apart from European support and the fact that many of the world's best players currently come from such a background, the other thing the World Matchplay has going for it is that McCormack still manages most of the world's best players and his organization still runs the event. Such a strong position will ensure the World Matchplay retains its high profile, perhaps even recovering some of its international prestige.

WORLD SERIES OF GOLF

Blessed with one of the sport's more evocative titles, the World Series of Golf is played every August at the Firestone Country Club in Akron, Ohio. Inaugurated in 1962, it began life as a 36-hole four man exhibition event, featuring the winners of each of the four major championships. It evolved in 1976 into a much more meaningful affair, with the field consisting of all of the winners of the United States Tour events for the previous 12 months, plus the winners of the most important tournaments held in other countries. In this way, the tournament allowed overseas golfers a taste of what life on the U.S. tour was like. Several European golfers, winners of eligible events such as the British PGA Championship or the European Open, gained all-too-rare experience of competing under American conditions.

Golf at Firestone began in the late 1920s, when Harvey Firestone laid out a course for the benefit of the employees at his Firestone tyre and rubber company. An enormous tee, complete with golf ball bearing the word 'Firestone' can be seen from all parts of the course, reminding visitors, if it be necessary, what the major industry is in this part of the world. Firestone held its first tour event in 1953, the appropriately titled Rubber City Open. This continued through until 1959, when the course was awarded the PGA Championship. Changes had to be made because the rather easy South Course was clearly not up to major champion-

Ben Crenshaw rates the World Series venue, Firestone, as one of world's toughest.

ship specifications. A recognized 'troubleshooter' in the form of Robert Trent Jones was called in. When Jones had finished adding 50 bunkers, two new ponds, and altering or rebuilding every green on the course, the venue had become the fearsome test of golf for which it is now renowned throughout the world.

Course for the Hitters

Its length of 7,180 yards makes it the longest on the tour, with a miserly par of just 70 strokes, and no less a luminary than Ben Crenshaw rates Firestone alongside Winged Foot, Oakmont and Royal Melbourne as one of the four toughest courses in the world. Just how difficult was emphasised in 1989 when Crenshaw lost a sudden death play-off for the title to the South African David Frost. Despite sublime conditions all week, the playing off total was 276 – just four under par. For all that, there has been some spectacular scoring, most notably by another South African Denis Watson, who shot a startling 62 during the second round of his winning year in 1984.

Since then the winners have been a motley bunch, with the names of Tom Watson and Curtis Strange sharing the trophy with the likes of Roger Maltbie and Dan Pohl. The tournament's capacity to surprise was probably best demonstrated in 1988 when Watson and Mike Reid were involved in a sudden death play-off. On the one hand you had one of the world's great players, for whom victory would have meant that he would have become the game's all-time leading money winner. On the other you had a player who earned his first $1 million before he won his first tournament, and one renowned as the shortest hitter on tour. Yes, you guessed it, Reid won, which proves, surely, that even on the longest courses accuracy and skill is as important as length.

Invariably, when the tiresome question of the 'fifth major championship' crops up, someone mentions the World Series of Golf. Certainly, the quality of its field each year earmarks it as one of the very best events in the world, a fact recognized by the tour, who grant the winner ten-year-exemption status. That is something that is handed out only to the three American majors plus one other tour event – the Players' Championship.

The most impressive performance in 1990 outside the majors was that of José-Maria Olazábal at the World Series. He won it by 11 shots.

INDEX